THE
BEST
AMERICAN
POETRY
1993

◊ ◊ ◊

OTHER VOLUMES IN THIS SERIES

THE
BEST
AMERICAN
POETRY
1993

◊ ◊ ◊

Louise Glück, Editor

David Lehman, Series Editor

COLLIER BOOKS

MACMILLAN PUBLISHING COMPANY

NEW YORK

MAXWELL MACMILLAN CANADA

TORONTO

MAXWELL MACMILLAN INTERNATIONAL

NEW YORK • OXFORD • SINGAPORE • SYDNEY

Collier Books
Macmillan Publishing Company
866 Third Avenue
New York, NY 10022

Maxwell Macmillan Canada, Inc.
1200 Eglinton Avenue East
Suite 200
Don Mills, Ontario M3C 3N1

Macmillan Publishing Company is part
of the Maxwell Communication Group of Companies.

ISBN 0-02-069846-1

ISSN 1040-5763

Macmillan Books are available at special discounts for bulk purchases
for sales promotions, premiums, fund-raising, or educational use.
For details, contact:
Special Sales Director
Macmillan Publishing Company
866 Third Avenue
New York, NY 10022

First Collier Books Edition 1993

10 9 8 7 6 5 4 3 2 1

Printed in the United States of America

CONTENTS

David Lehman was born in New York City in 1948. A graduate of Columbia and Cambridge universities, he has published two collections of poetry, *An Alternative to Speech* (1986) and *Operation Memory* (1990), both from Princeton University Press. The paperback edition of his book *Signs of the Times: Deconstruction and the Fall of Paul de Man* appeared in 1992 from Poseidon Press. His other books include *The Perfect Murder* (The Free Press, 1989) and *The Line Forms Here* (University of Michigan Press, 1992). He has taught at Hamilton College and has lectured in England, India, and Japan. He has received grants and prizes from the Guggenheim Foundation and the Ingram Merrill Foundation, and in 1991 was named a recipient of a three-year writer's award from the Lila Wallace–Reader's Digest Fund.

FOREWORD

by David Lehman

◊ ◊ ◊

Even an optimist on the subject of American poetry has days when
he wonders whether it's a losing cause—which for a romantic may
be the noblest cause worth fighting for. There are also days when,
in the words of Frank O'Hara, "I am ashamed of my century / for
being so entertaining / but I have to smile." One Wednesday last
May, Esther B. Fein of the *New York Times* reported in her "Book
Notes" column that John Ashbery had won the 1992 Ruth Lilly
Poetry Prize from *Poetry* magazine. On the same day, in the same
column, Fein passed along the news that Barbara Taylor Bradford,
a best-selling author of blockbuster fiction, had defected from
Random House to HarperCollins, a switch that—one wag later
exclaimed—"simultaneously raises the literary stature of both pub-
lishers." The thing that caught my eye in this juxtaposition of
publishing items was that Ashbery's prize included a purse of
$25,000, making it "one of the largest poetry awards in the United
States," while in spectacular contrast Bradford's new contract with
HarperCollins guaranteed her more than $20 million for her next
three poshlust potboilers. It was, in this context, refreshing to hear
what Ashbery told the *Times* reporter when she called him for a
quote. "Not that many people in this country like poetry," he said
matter-of-factly, "and in fact, many people hate it."

There is no need to deny the simple truth of this observation
even when affirming that, all in all, the climate for poetry in 1992
was more lovely and more temperate than the fickle weather of
Florida in August. There was even the occasional exception to the
rule that poetry and big bucks are mutually exclusive. The Nobel
Prize in literature—worth more than a million dollars—went to a
Caribbean poet, who divides his time between Boston and Trini-

dad. The announcement of Derek Walcott's good fortune, timed perfectly to coincide with the quincentennial of Columbus's expedition, raised to three the number of Nobel laureates who are primarily poets, were born elsewhere, live in the United States at least part of the time, and are published by Farrar, Straus & Giroux. More anomalous was the announcement, a few weeks before the Nobel news, that the same publisher had just sold the film rights to Elizabeth Bishop's "The Man-Moth." It's hard to predict what Columbia Pictures will do with its new property, since this terrific poem—which is based on a newspaper misprint—has no plot. Evidently, that is something the studio can provide. The producer and screenwriter are excited about the poem's atmosphere, which seems to them suggestive of "expressionist cinema." If the film is made, Bishop's forty-eight line poem could fetch as much as $75,000, or $1,562.50 per line.

Like cigarettes in fashion ads, poems are turning up in places where we stopped expecting to find them. At funkier-than-thou bars and cafés in cities from Boston to Los Angeles, teams of scruffy versifiers are slugging it out in mock-competitions known as poetry "slams." The poems aren't so much read as performed, like acts in a variety show, and the poet may be a bad-boy rapper, or a bad-girl tap dancer, or an unkempt bard with a goatee and a black turtleneck sweater playing the bass and howling. Are the beats back? No, the "wannabeats" have arrived. It is easy to mock the literary efforts on display, or to rue the transformation of the art into a species of nightclub infotainment suitable for MTV. But the whole "downtown" poetry phenomenon has felt a little like the gust of fresh air that turned into the blizzard of '93: a lot of noise, a lot of excitement, a lot of hype, and some rattling of the windows in stuffy rooms where another high-minded symposium on the future of poetry had been threatening to kill Pegasus and then beat the winged horse all over again.

Most of the good news concerning the publication of poetry has a modest pecuniary dimension. Given the economic conditions governing the book business during an extended recession, the wonder is not that some trade houses have abandoned poetry— which is the lamentable case—but that others have resolutely stayed with it and done reasonably well by it. But, then, the bottom line in this case is not financial at all. It is rather akin to the surprising last line in a sonnet of reversed expectations. It is the very plausible possibility that American poetry is, and should be, the envy of the English-speaking world—a statement made not with nationalistic fervor but with the pleasure and excitement that accompany creative ferment.

It may never be fashionable to admit this, but American poetry is not only in a state of high vitality but is reaching a wider public audience than pessimists ever thought possible. Ours may be a small audience by the standards of Barbara Taylor Bradford, a tiny audience by the standards of *Batman Returns* (which is, I think, what Hollywood means by "expressionist cinema"). But the audience for poetry is knowledgable and discriminating, avid to the point of love and dedication. It is also underrated in size. It is certainly an audience big enough to sustain the annual *Best American Poetry* anthology series, which is now six editions strong. Poetry, to paraphrase W. H. Auden, not only survives; it thrives in the valley of its saying.

The Best American Poetry is meant to be, in several senses, a state-of-the-art anthology. The selections are made each year by a different guest editor—in each case, a distinguished American poet—who reads many hundreds of poems culled from dozens of periodicals. John Ashbery, the guest editor of the inaugural volume, has been succeeded by Donald Hall, Jorie Graham, Mark Strand, Charles Simic, and this year, Louise Glück. Since she burst onto the scene with her first book *Firstborn* in 1968, when she was twenty-five years old, Ms. Glück has garnered accolades from the critics and honors and prizes from the institutions that award them. Her work holds a particular interest for other poets and for students of poetry. The poems in her last two books, *Ararat* and *The Wild Iris*, are dissimilar in style, subject matter, and focus. What they have in common is their urgency, their intensity, and the genuineness of their inspiration, which may be a hard quality to define but is an easy one to discern in poems that have a real authority.

The guest editors in this series have, without exception, been loyal to their lights and steadfast in their standards while ranging far afield in surveying the poetry of our time. People are curious about how the process works. It varies from year to year, but as a partner in the deliberations, I can attest that for the editors it is an awesome task to try to keep up with all the poetry out there—and it is always an educational experience. Both the guest editor and I find that we are constantly reading, and rereading, for the anthology. (Except for translations, all poems appearing in magazines in the year under survey are eligible.) Periodically, and with greater urgency as the year goes by, we compare notes, discoveries, enthusiasms, opinions. With some of the editors, the brunt of this work was done by phone; the letter was the medium of choice for Louise Glück, as it was for Donald Hall. Ms. Glück applied herself with vigor to the task of reading and evaluating poems. As the year began she could be heard clamoring for literary magazines "like a person in a restaurant banging the table for service." Devour them she did. Nearly four dozen magazines are represented in *The Best American Poetry 1993*, far more than in any previous year.

Putting the anthology together is a huge undertaking. The guest editor makes her final selections on New Year's Eve, revising the "yes list" (as we called it) for the last time that day. Now that the nucleus of the book is in place, we can go on to prepare the book's "backmatter." Each of the seventy-five poets has to be located, then asked (in some cases, cajoled) to supply biographical information and to comment on the chosen poem. Permissions have to be obtained. The editor's introduction and the series editor's foreword have to be written. The manuscript must be copy-edited, the galleys proofread with care. The cover art for the book must be chosen. And all this must be done in a great hurry, since our target date for finished books is Labor Day. It is a backbreaking production schedule, and this seems an opportune moment to thank the unheralded people—at the Macmillan Publishing Company and outside it—who collaborate on the project annually, making sure that no deadline is missed.

The Best American Poetry has a primary purpose, announced in its title—to honor poems of immediate interest and enduring value—but also several subsidiary purposes, such as the desire to feed the interest that readers of poetry are bound to have in the taste and judgment of our leading poets. It is true, as several persons have said, that the title of this book makes an aggressive claim. That is one reason why I like it. I like the idea of risking an unequivocal opinion. (As former President Jimmy Carter—who published three of his poems last year in *New Letters*—put it: Why not the best?) Working on the book generates an almost palpable sense of excitement as each year's guest editor begins with a certain healthy skepticism—are there really as many as seventy-five poems out there worthy of inclusion?—and concludes the task complaining that seventy-five is too low a limit. Though the hours are long and the labor sometimes wearying, there is a special pleasure in challenging a shibboleth, and it continues to be fun proving that poets of various camps, schools, movements, and regions can consort to their mutual advantage, to the reader's edification, to the editors' delight, and to everyone's profit. Long may it be so.

Louise Glück was born in New York City in 1943. She grew up on Long Island. In 1968 she published her first book of poetry, *Firstborn*. Her other books include *The House on Marshland* (1975), *Descending Figure* (1980), and *Ararat* (1990), all from the Ecco Press. *The Triumph of Achilles* (Ecco, 1985) won the National Book Critics Circle Award. *The Wild Iris*, her sixth collection, appeared from Ecco in 1992 and went on to win the Pulitzer Prize. Currently on the faculty of Williams College, Ms. Glück has taught at Columbia University, the University of Iowa, Berkeley, and UCLA, and has received grants from the Guggenheim Foundation, the Rockefeller Foundation, and the National Endowment for the Arts. She delivered the Phi Beta Kappa poem at Harvard in 1990. In 1992 she and Mark Strand were named corecipients of the biennial Rebekah Johnson Bobbitt National Prize for poetry, given at the Library of Congress. She recently completed a book of essays to be published by the Ecco Press. She lives in Plainfield, Vermont, with her husband and son.

INTRODUCTION

by Louise Glück

◇　◇　◇

The world is complete without us. Intolerable fact. To which the poet responds by rebelling, wanting to prove otherwise. Out of wounded vanity or stubborn pride or desolate need, the poet lives in chronic dispute with fact, and an astonishment occurs: another fact is created, like a new element, in partial contradiction of the intolerable. Indelible voice, though it has no impact on the nonhuman universe, profoundly alters our experience of that universe as well as of the world of human relations; to all that is most solitary in our natures, it is the sustaining companion.

We know this happens: literature is its record or testament. A chilling word, literature. It lacks all sense of the voice's adamant vitality. As an abstraction, it converts the poem into something equally disembodied, a resolved thing, inert and distant. Whereas the voice that rises from the page is weirdly restless: seductive, demanding, embittered, witty. Speaking not from the past but in the present. And it still occurs: voices emerge from which, in Robinson Jeffers's phrase, fire cannot be leeched, whether because cultural shifts create them or because they enact the ancient dispute with new emphasis or because there is in them some quality or force not yet identified.

It would be interesting to know something about that quality, because the poem, no matter how charged its content, survives not through content but through voice. By voice I mean style of thought, for which a style of speech—the clever grafts and borrowings, the habitual gestures scattered like clues in the lines— never convincingly substitutes. We fall back on that term, *voice,* for all its insufficiencies; it suggests, at least, the sound of an authentic being. Although such sound may draw on the poet's actual manner of speech, it is not, on the page, transcription. The voice is at liberty to excerpt, to exaggerate, to bypass what it chooses, to issue from conditions the real world will never exactly reproduce; unlike speech, it bears no immediate social pressure, since the other to whom it strives to make itself clear may not yet exist. The poem means to create that person, first in the poet, then in the reader. Meanwhile, its fidelity is not to external reality: it need not provide a replica of the outward, or of social relations. This is why time confers more readily on the apolitical novel political significance: nineteenth-century romantic novels, for example, were not necessarily conceived as political statements; they become such statements in light of a contemporary readiness to politicize gender relations. The novel seems oddly easier on many readers, who are puzzled by the poem's independence, puzzled, even, by the voice's unnerving authenticity. The conviction that poems must be autobiography (since they are not description) begins here, in the reader's belief that the actual and the true are synonyms.

Poems *are* autobiography, but divested of the trappings of chronology and comment, the metronomic alternation of anecdote and response. Moreover, a body of work may change and develop less in reaction to the lived life than in reaction to the poet's prior discoveries, or the discoveries of others. If a poem remains so selectively amplified, so casual with fact, as to seem elusive, we must remember its agenda: not, or not simply, to record the actual but to continously create the sensation of immersion in the actual. And if, in its striving to be free of the imprisoning self, the poet's gaze trains itself outward, it rests nevertheless on what compels or arrests it. Such choices constitute a portrait. Where the gaze is held, voice, or response, begins. Always in what follows the poet is alert, resistant, resisting dogma and fashion, resisting the greater danger of personal conviction, which must be held suspect, given its resemblance to dogma.

Still, for poems to touch us, we have to be magnetically drawn, we have to want to read these things. What makes this possible, what are the characteristics of those voices that, even as they become epigraphs or inscriptions on stone, mock the stone and the page with their vitality? Not, I think, that they sound beautiful or speak truth. Of these claims, the second seems at once grander and more accessible because of the ease with which truth identifies itself with sincerity as opposed to insight. Art's truth is as different from sincerity's honest disclosure as it is different from the truth administered in the doctor's office, that sequence of knowns which the doctor, newly trained to respect the patient's dignity, makes wholly available, affording, in the process, glimpses into a world of probabilities and strategies, the world of action transposed to conditions in which action can do only so much. The poem may embody perception so luminous it seems truth, but what keeps it alive is not fixed discovery but the means to discovery; what keeps it alive is intelligence.

No one disputes the desirability of intelligence. Many afternoons on the playground are ruined by assertions of its lack, many mornings in the charged classroom. The question is, how does it manifest itself, how does investment in truth constrain it?

The second issue first. Art is not a service. Or, rather, it does not reliably serve all people in a standardized way. Its service is to the spirit, from which it removes the misery of inertia. It does this by refocusing an existing image of the world; in this sense, it is less mirror than microscope—where the flat white of the page was, a field of energy emerges. Nevertheless, the absence of social function or social usefulness sometimes combines in the poet with a desire to serve, to do good. This absence and this pressure direct the poet toward the didactic. The teacherly, the wise, the morally sound, the noble: such utterance further soothes the poet's fragile ego by seeming to align his or her voice with the great voices, whose perceptions have been internalized as truth. But to make vital art, the poet must forswear this alliance, however desperately it is sought, since what it produces is reiteration. Which is to say, not perception, but the homage that simulates what it cannot generate. Not the arrow, but the stained garment. And what is inevitably missing from such reiteration is the sense of speech issuing in the moment from a specific, identifiable voice; what is missing is the sense of immediacy, volatility, which gives such voices their paradoxical durability. Whatever the nature of these voices, wherever they occur on the continuum between the casual and delphic, insight, as they speak it, feels like shocking event: wholly absent and then inevitable. And it comes slyly, or with an air of being unwilled, the air of query or postulate or vision.

In the reader, at these moments, an idea is being attacked, and the attack exhilarates. The old idea, not so much formulated as tacitly assumed, in its unclarity neither recognized nor repudiated, is displaced by perception. So the actively felt rushes to displace the passively unexamined, unsettling everything built on that ground, and the air turns giddy with possibility, as though a whole new territory in the mind had been suddenly opened. Nothing has been destroyed that continues to be prized—rather, space is added. What has been sacrificed or shed seems only opacity, a sluggish dullness. Even when the sensation that one's solitude is shared disappears, what remains suggests solitude's fecundity.

As for the poet: mere unease, mere doubting of received ideas, is never enough: the poem must, on whatever scale, dislodge assumption, not by simply opposing it, but by dismantling the systematic proof on which its inevitability depends. In other words: not "C is wrong" but "who says A has to lead to B?" High seriousness, in its common disguise as tedious sobriety, is one of intelligence's readiest targets.

The poem that mistakes noble utterance for perception, conviction for impassioned intelligence, has located a wisdom it means to confer on its readers. Although such a poem may be organized dramatically and will likely have its climactic moment, it lacks drama: one feels, too early, its intention. Nor does deep familiarity with its design suggest that the poem has tapped into myth: myth is not formula. Such poems substitute the adjective for the noun; they offer the world draped in mythic reference. But in their willfulness, they lack myth's fatedness, myth's helpless encounter with the elemental. Instead, everything has been invested in conclusion, in axiom, in heroic grandeur. Poetic intelligence lacks, I think, such focused investment in conclusion, being naturally wary of its own assumptions. It derives its energy from a willingness to discard conclusions in the face of evidence, its willingness, in fact, to discard anything.

This flexibility and this intensity of purpose give the sort of eerie steadiness of mind Emily Dickinson has. Even poets who stray wildly, intentionally, display such steadiness, since its essence is attentiveness to the path of thought. Nor is this egotism: thought, liberated of preconception, has nothing to do with self. What self is so free as to be able to disdain all previously held belief? Great concentration is required: perception does not hold still, patiently waiting to be encircled and made famous. It is visible in part, in moments; like the particles at the end of the microscope, it moves.

The voice that never existed can issue only from the life that never existed, a life experienced (whether it be adventurous or hermetic) wholly and without sentimental simplification, the enduring general deriving continually from the accepted individual life.

I took on this project for three reasons. First, I was impressed by David Lehman's willingness to let me say a few words against it. Second, I thought it would be wholesome to actually read, for a year, everything published in American magazines; conceivably, information would check my tendency to generalization and wild hypothesis. Last, I recognized, in my habitual refusal of this sort of assignment, a kind of preening. I preferred the cleanliness of powerlessness, but the refusal of power differs from lack of power; it places one among that elect to whom a choice is given. This particular mode, this life on the sidelines, preferably the very front of the sidelines, with the best view of the errors of others, promotes feelings of deeply satisfying moral rectitude combined with an invigorating sense of injustice: the particular limitations and insufficiencies and blindnesses of one's own preferences are never exposed because those preferences are never enacted. I liked not participating in the tyranny of taste making; I liked used words like "tyranny" and "taste making" to describe enacted preference, while guarding for myself words like "purity." What disrupts this is whatever offer finally makes clear the conditions on which refusal is based. I continue to feel aversion to overt authority, but a moment arrived in which I could no longer persuade myself that avoidance and lack were the same: they differ as willed and unwilled differ, as Marie Antoinette differs from the real milkmaid; continuous refusal to exert public influence on behalf of what I valued, like continuous refusal to expose my judgment to public scrutiny, seemed vanity and self protection.

Meanwhile, unease lingers, in part a response to terminology. I dislike the idea that a single mind, or even a collective bound together by a common theory, should determine what is called best. As critics have observed, the poets themselves decide this, over time; the great ones are those to whom the poets repeatedly return. The point here is the diversity of that plural noun. And the fact of time, which purges these judgments of all trace of personality and allows, as well, for the disruption of one conservatism by another. If we are not necessarily the best readers of what is written in our own time, how can we assume that excellence always finds its way into print? Finally, I think poets are not served by the existence of another mechanism of ranking, however sweet recognition may seem. Hierarchy dissolves passionate fellowship into bitter watch-fulness—those who aren't vulnerable are usually those who are regularly honored. What is essential is that we sustain our readiness to learn from each other, a readiness that, by definition, requires from each of us the best work possible. We must, I think, fear whatever erodes the generosity on which exacting criticism depends.

Some of these reservations have been countered by the pleasure of discovery; some of this criticism checked by new awe for editors of magazines: every year they do what I did for one year. The miracle is not that they miss something but that they find so much.

I tried to read with perfect detachment and could not. Inevitably, we read best the work that seems absolutely fresh, or the work of those poets whose oeuvres we know thoroughly—such knowledge provides a resonance which cannot help but inform the reading of any single poem. On the other hand, such knowledge does not proceed from indifference: it presumes interest. I faltered in other ways; I read most clearly at the beginning, before I began drowning. As for the tonic effects of this labor: the mind that inclines to paradigm needs more than a year's comprehensive reading to correct its bias.

This collection is limited to what was published in one year, in magazines. Which creates regrettable omissions: this book should not be regarded as an anthology of the memorable work of our period, but as a culling, a journal of twelve months. I tried to be open-minded; my hope was to have my mind changed. I was equally determined, in any choice between two poems of equal interest, to favor the work of the less well-known writer. That the anthology, as it stands, is not particularly iconoclastic attests to my previously scattered reading in contemporary poetry: any number of poets unknown to me proved neither unknown nor unsung, as their biographies make clear. Also, perhaps hearteningly, poets of great reputation turn out, with some frequency, to produce remarkable poems.

I still prefer teaching as a means to encounter the not fully real-ized, the sporadically wonderful. That context transforms the unre-alized to the incipient. The magazines I read regularly offer examples of the extremely interesting, the very nearly remarkable. But the teacher meets such poems as mutable forms, for which no destiny seems impossible.

And yet, among the many poems I read—the poems inaccessible to me, the poems that were echoes of other poems, the poems of startling promise—there were voices that stood out, like the voice at the dinner table whose next sentence you strain to hear, and some of these may prove unforgettable.

THE
BEST
AMERICAN
POETRY
1993

◊ ◊ ◊

Garbage

◊   ◊   ◊

I

Creepy little creepers are insinuatingly
curling up my spine (bringing the message)

saying, Boy!, are you writing that great poem
the world's waiting for: don't you know you

have an unaccomplished mission unaccomplished;
someone somewhere may be at this very moment

dying for the lack of what W. C. Williams says
you could (or somebody could) be giving: yeah?

so, these messengers say, what do you
mean teaching school (teaching *poetry* and

poetry writing and wasting your time painting
sober little organic, meaningful pictures)

when values thought lost (but only scrambled into
disengagement) lie around demolished

and centerless because you (that's me, boy)
haven't elaborated everything in everybody's

face, yet: on the other hand (I say to myself,
receiving the messengers and cutting them down)

who has done anything or am I likely to do
anything the world won't twirl without: and

since SS's enough money (I hope) to live
from now on on in elegance and simplicity—

or, maybe, just simplicity—why shouldn't I
at my age (63) concentrate on chucking the

advancements and rehearsing the sweetnesses of
leisure, nonchalance, and small-time byways: couple

months ago, for example, I went all the way
from soy flakes (already roasted and pressed

and in need of an hour's simmering boil
to be cooked) all the way to soybeans, the

pure golden pearls themselves, 65¢ lb. dry: they
have to be soaked overnight in water and they

have to be boiled slowly for six hours—but
they're welfare cheap, are a complete protein,

more protein by weight than meat, more
calcium than milk, more lecithin than eggs,

and somewhere in there the oil that smoothes
stools, a great virtue: I need time and verve

to find out, now, about medicare/medicaid,
national osteoporosis week, gadabout tours,

hearing loss, homesharing programs, and choosing
good nutrition! for starters! why should I

be trying to write my flattest poem, now, for
whom, not for myself, for others?, posh, as I

have never said: Social Security can provide
the beans, soys enough: my house, paid for for

twenty years, is paid for: my young'un
is raised: nothing one can pay cash for seems

very valuable: that reaches a high enough
benchmark for me—high enough that I wouldn't

know what to do with anything beyond that, no
place to house it, park it, dock it, let it drift

down to: elegance and simplicity: I wonder
if we need those celestial guidance systems

striking mountaintops or if we need fuzzy
philosophy's abstruse failed reasonings: isn't

it simple and elegant enough to believe in
qualities, simplicity and elegance, pitch in a

little courage and generosity, a touch of
commitment, enough asceticism to prevent

fattening: moderation: elegant and simple
moderation: trees defined themselves (into

various definitions) through a dynamics of
struggle (hey, is the palaver rapping, yet?)

and so it is as if there were a genetic
recognition that a young tree would get up and

through only through taken space (parental
space not yielding at all, either) and, further:

so, trunks, accommodated to rising, to reaching
the high light and deep water, were slender

and fast moving, and this was okay because
one good thing about dense competition is that

if one succeeds with it one is buttressed by
crowding competitors; that is, there was little

room for branches, and just a tuft of green
possibility at the forest's roof: but, now,

I mean, take my yard maple—put out in the free
and open—has overgrown, its trunk

split down from a high fork: wind has
twisted off the biggest, bottom branch: there

was, in fact, hardly any crowding and competition,
and the fat tree, unable to stop pouring it on,

overfed and overgrew and, now, again, its skin's
broken into and disease may find it and bores

of one kind or another, and fungus: it just
goes to show you: moderation imposed is better

than no moderation at all: we tie into the
lives of those we love and our lives, then, go

as theirs go; their pain we can't shake off;
their choices, often harming to themselves,

pour through our agitated sleep, swirl up as
no-nos in our dreams; we rise several times

in a night to walk about; we rise in the morning
to a crusty world headed nowhere, doorless:

our chests burn with anxiety and a river of
anguish defines rapids and straits in the pit of

our stomachs: how can we intercede and not
interfere: how can our love move more surroundingly,

convincingly than our premonitory advice

II

garbage has to be the poem of our time because
garbage is spiritual, believable enough

to get our attention, getting in the way, piling
up, stinking, turning brooks brownish and

creamy white: what else deflects us from the
errors of our illusionary ways, not a temptation

to trashlessness, that is too far off, and,
anyway, unimaginable, unrealistic: I'm a

hole puncher or hole plugger: stick a finger
in the dame (*dam*, damn, dike), hold back the issue

of creativity's flood, the forthcoming, futuristic,
the origins feeding trash: down by I-95 in

Florida where flat land's ocean-and gulf-flat,
mounds of disposal rise (for if you dug

something up to make room for something to put
in, what about the something dug up, as with graves:)

the garbage trucks crawl as if in obeisance,
as if up ziggurats toward the high places gulls

and garbage keep alive, offerings to the gods
of garbage, of retribution, of realistic

expectation, the deities of unpleasant
necessities: refined, young earthworms,

drowned up in macadam pools by spring rains, moisten
out white in a day or so and, round spots,

look like sputum or creamy-rich, broken-up cold
clams: if this is not the best poem of the

century, can it be about the worst poem of the
century: it comes, at least, toward the end,

so a long tracing of bad stuff can swell
under its measure: but there on the heights

a small smoke wafts the sacrificial bounty
day and night to layer the sky brown, shut us

in as into a lidded kettle, the everlasting
flame these acres-deep of tendance keep: a

free offering of a crippled plastic chair:
a played-out sports outfit: a hill-myna

print stained with jelly: how to write this
poem, should it be short, a small popping of

duplexes, or long, hunting wide, coming home
late, losing the trail and recovering it:

should it act itself out, illustrations,
examples, colors, clothes or intensify

reductively into statement, bones any corpus
would do to surround, or should it be nothing

at all unless it finds itself: the poem,
which is about the pre-socratic idea of the

dispositional axis from stone to wind, wind
to stone (with my elaborations, if any)

is complete before it begins, so I needn't
myself hurry into brevity, though a weary reader

might briefly be done: the axis will be clear
enough daubed here and there with a little ink

or fined out into every shade and form of its
revelation: this is a scientific poem,

asserting that nature models values, that we
have invented little (copied), reflections of

possibilities already here, this where we came
to and how we came: a priestly director behind the

black-chuffing dozer leans the gleanings and
reads the birds, millions of loners circling

a common height, alighting to the meaty steaks
and puffy muffins (puffins?): there is a mound

too, in the poet's mind dead language is hauled
off to and burned down on, the energy held and

shaped into new turns and clusters, the mind
strengthened by what it strengthens for

where but in the very asshole of come-down is
redemption: as where but brought low, where

but in the grief of failure, loss, error do we
discern the savage afflictions that turn us around:

---

where but in the arrangements love crawls us
through, not a thing left in our self-display

unhumiliated, do we find the sweet seed of
new routes: but we are natural: nature, not

we, gave rise to us: we are not, though, though
natural, divorced from higher, finer configurations:

tissues and holograms and energy circulate in
us and seek and find representations of themselves

outside us, so that we can participate in
celebrations high and know reaches of feeling

and sight and thought that penetrate (really
penetrate) far, far beyond these our wet cells,

right on up past our stories, the planets, moons,
and other bodies locally to the other end of

the pole where matter's forms diffuse and
energy loses all means to express itself except

as spirit, there, oh, yes, in the abiding where
mind but nothing else abides, the eternal,

until it turns into another pear or sunfish,
that momentary glint in the fisheye having

been there so long, coming and going, it's
eternity's glint: it all wraps back round,

into and out of form, palpable and impalpable,
and in one phase, the one of grief and love,

we know the other, where everlastingness comes to
sway, okay and smooth: the heaven we mostly

want, though, is this jet-hoveled hell back,
heaven's daunting asshole: one must write and

rewrite till one writes it right: if I'm in
touch, she said, then I've got an edge: what

the hell kind of talk is that: I can't believe
I'm merely an old person: whose mother is dead,

whose father is gone and many of whose
friends and associates have wended away to the

ground, which is only heavy wind, or to ashes,
a lighter breeze: but it was all quite frankly

to be expected and not looked forward to: even
old trees, I remember some of them, where they

used to stand: pictures taken by some of them:
and old dogs, specially one imperial black one,

quad dogs with their hier*archies* (another *archie*)
one succeeding another, the barking and romping

sliding away like slides from a projector: what
were they then that are what they are now:

III

toxic waste, poison air, beach goo, eroded
roads draw nations together, whereas magnanimous

platitude and sweet semblance ease each nation
back into its comfort or despair: global crises

promote internationalist gettings-together,
problems the best procedure, whether they be in the

poet warps whose energy must be found and let
work or in the high windings of sulfur dioxide:

I say to my writing students—prize your flaws,
defects, behold your accidents, engage your

negative criticisms—these are the materials
of your ongoing—from these places you imagine,

find, or make the ways back to all of us, the figure,
keeping the aberrant periphery worked

clear so the central current may shift or slow
or rouse adjusting to the necessary dynamic:

in our error the defining energies of cure
errancy finds: suffering otherwises: but

no use to linger over beauty or simple effect:
this is just a poem with a job to do: and that

is to declare, however roundabout, sideways,
or meanderingly (or in those ways) the perfect

scientific and materialistic notion of the
spindle of energy: when energy is gross,

rocklike, it resembles the gross, and when
fine it mists away into mystical refinements,

sometimes passes right out of material
recognizability and becomes, what?, motion,

spirit, all forms translated into energy, as at
the bottom of Dante's hell all motion is

translated into form: so, in value systems,
physical systems, artistic systems, always this

same disposition from the heavy to the light,
and then the returns from the light downward

to the staid gross: stone to wind, wind to
stone: there is no need for "outside," hegemonic

derivations of value: nothing need be invented
or imposed: the aesthetic, scientific, moral

are organized like a muff along this spindle,
might as well relax: thus, the job done, the

mind having found its way through and marked
out the course, the intellect can be put by:

one can turn to tongue, crotch, boob, navel,
armpit, rock, slit, roseate rearend and

consider the perfumeries of slick exchange,
heaving breath, slouchy mouth, the mixed

means by which we stay attentive and keep to
the round of our ongoing: you wake up thrown

away and accommodation becomes the name of your
game: getting back, back into the structure

of protection, caring, warmth, numbers: one
and many, singles and groups, dissensions and

cooperations, takings and givings—the dynamic
of survival, still the same: but why thrown

out in the first place: because while the
prodigal stamps off and returns, the father goes

from iron directives that drove the son away
to rejoicing tears at his return: the safe

world of community, not safe, still needs
feelers sent out to test the environment, to

bring back news or no news; the central
mover, the huge river, needs, too, to bend,

and the son sent away is doubly welcomed home:
we deprive ourselves of, renounce, safety to seek

greater safety: but if we furnish a divine
sanction or theology to the disposition, we

must not think when the divine sanction shifts
that there is any alteration in the disposition:

the new's an angle of emphasis on the old:
new religions are surfaces, beliefs the shadows

of images trying to construe what needs no
belief: only born die, and if something is

born or new, then that is not it, that is not
the it: the it is the indifference of all the

differences, the nothingness of all the poised
somethings, the finest issue of energy in which

boulders and dead stars float: for what
if it were otherwise and the it turned out to

be *something*, damning and demanding, strict and
fierce, preventing and seizing: what range of

choice would be given up then and what value
could our partial, remnant choices acquire then:

with a high whine the garbage trucks slowly
circling the pyramid rising intone the morning

and atop the mound's plateau birds circling
hear and roil alive in winklings of wings

denser than windy forest shelves: and meanwhile
a truck already arrived spills its goods from

the back hatch and the birds as in a single computer
formed net plunge in celebrations, hallelujahs

of rejoicing: the driver gets out of his truck
and wanders over to the cliff on the spill and

looks off from the high point into the rosy-fine
rising of day, the air pure, the wings of the

birds white and clean as angel-food cake: holy, holy,
holy, the driver cries and flicks his cigarette

in a spiritual swoop that floats and floats before
it touches ground: here, the driver knows,

where the consummations gather, where the disposal
flows out of form, where the last translations

cast away their immutable bits and scraps,
flits of steel, shivers of bottle and tumbler,

here is the gateway to beginning, here the portal
of renewing change, the birdshit, even, melding

enrichingly in with debris, a loam for the roots
of placenta: oh, nature, the man on the edge

of the cardboard-laced cliff exclaims, that there
could be a straightaway from the toxic past into

the fusion-lit reaches of a coming time! our
sins are so many, here heaped, shapes given to

false matter, hamburger meat left out

IV

scientists plunge into matter looking for the
matter but the matter lessens and, looked too

far into, expands away: it was insubstantial all
along: that is, boulders bestir; they

are "alive" with motion and space: there is a
riddling reality where real hands grasp each

other in the muff but toward both extremes the
reality wears out, wears thin, becomes a reality

"realityless": this is satisfactory, providing
permanent movement and staying, providing the

stratum essential with an essential air, the
poles thick and thin, the middles, at interchange:

the spreader rakes a furrow open and lights a
drying edge: a priestly plume rises, a signal, smoke

like flies intermediating between orange peel
and buzzing blur: is a poem about garbage garbage

or will this abstract, hollow junk seem beautiful
and necessary as just another offering to the

high assimilations: (that means up on top where
the smoke is; the incinerations of sin,

corruption, misconstruction pass through the
purification of flame:) old deck chairs,

crippled aluminum lawn chairs, lemon crates
with busted slats or hinges, strollers with

whacking or spinningly idle wheels: stub ends
of hot dogs: clumps go out; rain sulls deep

coals; wind slams flickers so flat they lose
the upstanding of updraft and stifle to white

lingo—but oh, oh, in a sense, and in an
intention, the burning's forever, O eternal

flame, principle of the universe, without which
mere heaviness and gray rust prevail: dance

peopling the centers and distances, the faraway
galactic slurs even, luminescences, plasmas,

those burns, the same principle: but here on
the heights, terns and flies avoid the closest

precincts of flame, the terrifying transformations,
the disappearances of anything of interest,

morsel, gobbet, trace of maple syrup, fat
worm: addling intensity at the center

where only special clothes and designated
offices allay the risk, the pure center: but

down, down on the lowest appropinquations, the
laborsome, loaded vessels whine like sails in

too much wind up the long ledges, the whines
a harmony, singing away the end of the world

or spelling it in, a monstrous surrounding of
gathering—the putrid, the castoff, the used,

the mucked up—all arriving for final assessment,
for the toting up in tonnage, the separations

of wet and dry, returnable and gone for good:
the sanctifications, the burn-throughs, ash free

merely a permanent twang of light, a dwelling
music, remaining: how to be blessed are mechanisms,

procedures that carry such changes! the
garbage spreader gets off his bulldozer and

approaches the fire: he stares into it as into
eternity, the burning edge of beginning and

ending, the catalyst of going and becoming,
and all thoughts of his paycheck and beerbelly,

even all thoughts of his house and family and
the long way he has come to be worthy of his

watch, fall away, and he stands in the presence
of the momentarily everlasting, the air about

him sacrosanct, purged of the crawling vines
and dense vegetation of desire, nothing between

perception and consequence here: the arctic
terns move away from the still machine and

light strikes their wings in round, a fluttering,
a whirling rose of wings, and it seems that

terns' slender wings and finely tipped
tails look so airy and yet so capable that they

must have been designed after angels or angels
after them: the lizard family produced man in

the winged air! man as what he might be or might
have been, neuter, guileless, a feathery hymn:

the bulldozer man picks up a red bottle that
turns purple and green in the light and pours

out a few drops of stale wine, and yellow jackets
burr in the bottle, sung drunk, the singing

not even puzzled when he tosses the bottle way
down the slopes, the still air being flown in

in the bottle even as the bottle dives through
the air! the bulldozer man thinks about that

and concludes that everything is marvelous, what
he should conclude and what everything is: on

the deepdown slopes, he realizes, the light
inside the bottle will, over the weeks, change

the yellow jackets, unharmed, having left lost,
not an aromatic vapor of wine left, the air

percolating into and out of the neck as the sun's
heat rises and falls: all is one, one all:

hallelujah: he gets back up on his bulldozer
and shaking his locks backs the bulldozer up

V

dew shatters into rivulets on crunched cellophane
as the newly started bulldozer jars a furrow

off the mesa, smoothing and packing down:
flattening, the way combers break flat into

speed up the strand: unpleasant food strings down
the slopes and rats' hard tails whirl whacking

trash: I don't know anything much about garbage
dumps: I mean, I've never climbed one: I

don't know about the smells: do masks mask
scent: or is there a deodorizing mask: the

Commissioner of Sanitation in a bug-black caddy
hearse-long glisters creepy up the ziggurat: at

the top his chauffeur pops out and opens the
big back door for him: he goes over a few feet

away, puts a stiff, salute-hand to his forehead
and surveys the distances in all depths: the

birds' shadows lace his white sleeve: he
rises to his toes as a lifting zephyr from the

sea lofts a salt-shelf of scent: he approves: he
extends his arm in salute to the noisy dozer's

operator, waves back and forth canceling out
any intention to speak, re-beholds Florida's

longest vistas, gets back into the big buggy
and runs up all the windows, trapping, though,

a nuisance of flies: (or, would he have run
the windows down: or would anyone else have:

not out there: strike that:) rightness, at
any rate, like a benediction, settles on the

ambiance: all is proceeding: funding will be
continued: this work will not be abandoned:

this mound can rise higher: things are in order
when heights are acknowledged; the lows

ease into place; the wives get back from the laundromat,
the husbands hose down the hubcaps; and the

seeringly blank pressures of weekends crack
away hour by hour in established time: in your

end is my beginning: the operator waves back
to the Commissioner, acknowledging his understanding

and his submission to benign authority, and falls
to thinking of his wife, née Minnie Furher, a woman

of abrupt appetites and strict morals, a woman
who wants what she wants legally, largely as a

function of her husband's particulars: a closet
queen, Minnie hides her cardboard, gold-foiled

crown to wear in parade about the house when
nobody's home: she is so fat, fat people

like to be near her: and her husband loves
every bit of her, every bite (bit) round enough to get

to: and wherever his dinky won't reach, he finds
something else that will: I went up the road

a piece this morning at ten to Pleasant Grove
for the burial of Ted's ashes: those above

ground care; those below don't: the sun was
terribly hot, and the words of poems read out

loud settled down like minnows in a shallows
for the moment of silence and had their gaps

and fractures filled up and healed quiet: into
the posthole went the irises and hand-holds of dirt:

spring brings thaw and thaw brings the counterforce
of planted ashes which may not rise again,

not as anything recognizable as what they leach
away from: oh, yes, yes, the matter goes on,

turning into this and that, never the same thing
twice: but what about the spirit, does it die

in an instant, being nothing in an instant out of
matter, or does it hold on to some measure of

time, not just the eternity in which it is not,
but does death go on being death for a billion

years: this one fact put down is put down
forever, is it, or forever, forever to be a

part of the changes about it, switches in the
earth's magnetic field, asteroid collisions,

tectonic underplays, to be molten and then not
molten, again and again: when does a fact end:

what does one do with this gap from just yesterday
or just this morning to fifty-five billion

years—to infinity: the spirit was forever
and is forever, the residual and informing

energy, but here what concerns us is this
manifestation, this man, this incredible flavoring and

building up of character and éclat, gone,
though forever, in a moment only, a local

event, infinitely unrepeatable: the song of
the words subsides, the shallows drift away,

the people turn to each other and away: motors
start and the driveways clear, and the single

fact is left alone to itself to have its first
night under the stars but to be there now

for every star that comes: we go away who must
ourselves come back, at last to stay: tears

when we are helpless are our only joy: but
while I was away this morning, Mike, the young

kid who does things for us, cut down the
thrift with his weedeater, those little white

flowers more like weedsize more than likely:
sometimes called cliff rose: also got the grass

out of the front ditch now too wet to mow, slashed:
the dispositional axis is not supreme (how tedious)

and not a fiction (how clever) but plain (greatness
flows through the lowly) and a fact (like as not)

from *American Poetry Review*

Baked Alaska

◇ ◇ ◇

I

It will do. It's not
perfect, but it will do
until something better comes along.

It's not perfect.
It stinks. How are we
going to get out of having it
until something comes along, some ride
or other? That will return us
to the nominative case, shipshape and easy.

O but how long are you going to wait
for what you are waiting for, for
whatever is to come? Not
for long, you may be sure.
It may be here already.
Have you checked the mailbox today?

Sure I have, but listen.
I know what comes, comes.
I am prepared
to occupy my share of days,
knowing I can't have all of them. What is, is
coming over here to find you
missing, all or in part. Or you read me

one small item out of the newspaper
as though it would stand for today.
I refuse to open your box of crayons. Oh yes, I know
there may be something new in some combination
of styles, some gift in adding the addled
colors to our pate. But it's just too mush
for me. It isn't that I necessarily
set out on the trail of a new theory
that could liberate us from our shoes as we walked.
It's rather that the apartment comes to an end
in a small, pinched frown of shadow. He walked
through the wood, as a child. He will walk
on somebody's street in the days that come after.
He's noted as a problem child, an ignoramus;
therefore why can you not accept him in
your arms, girdled with silver-and-black
orchids, feed him everyday food?

Who says he likes cuttlebone?
But you get the idea, the idea
is to humor him for what vexations
may hatch from the stone attitude
that follows and clears the head, like a sneeze.
It's cozy to cuddle up to him,
not so much for warmth as that brains
are scarce, and two will have to do.
It takes two to tango,
it is written, and much
in the way of dragon's teeth after that,
and then the ad-hoc population that arises
on stilts, ready to greet or destroy us, it
doesn't matter which, not quite yet, at least.

Then when the spent avenger
turns tail you know it had all to do with
you, that discharge of fortunes
out of firecrackers, like farts. And who's to say
you don't get the one that belongs to you?

But he speaks, always, in terms of perfection,
of what we were going to have
if only he hadn't gotten busy and done something
    about it, yea,
and turned us back into ourselves
with something missing. And as oarsmen
paddle a scull downstream with phenomenal speed,
so he, in his cape, queries:
Is the last one all right? I know
I keep speaking of the last one, but is it all right?
For only after an infinite series
has eluded us does the portrait
of the boy make sense, and then such a triangular one:
he might have been a minaret, or a seagull.
He laid that on the car's radiator
and when you turned around it is gone.

II

Some time later, in Provence,
you waxed enthusiastic about the tail-
piece in a book, gosh how they
don't make them like that in this century, anymore.
They had a fibre then that doesn't exist now.
That's all you can do about it.
Sensing this, in the sopping diaspora, many a tanglefoot
waits, stars bloom at scalloped edges
of no thing, and it begins to
bleed, like a bomb or bordello.
The theme, unscathed,
with nothing to attach it to.

But like I was saying, probably some of us were
    encouraged
by a momentary freshness in the air
that proved attractive, once we had dwelt in

it, and bathed for many years our temples in its essence.
   Listen, memory:
Do this one thing for me
and I'll never ask you again for anything else—
just tell me how it began! What
were the weeds that got caught in the spokes
as it was starting up, the time the brake shaft split,
and what about all the little monsters that were willing to sit
on the top of your tit, or index finger.
How in the end sunshine prevailed—
but what was that welling in between?
Those bubbles
that proceeded from nowhere—surely there must be a
   source?
Because if there isn't it means that we haven't paid
for this ticket, and will be stopped at the exit gate
and sent back on a return journey through plowed fields
to not necessarily the starting place, that house
we can hardly remember, with the plangent
rose-patterned curtains.

And so in turn he who gets locked up is lost,
too, and must watch a boat nudge the pier
outside his window, forever, and for aye,
and the nose, the throat will be stopped
by absolutely correct memories of what did
we think we were doing when it all began happening,
down the lanes, across vales, out into the open city street.

And those it chooses can always say
it's easy, once you learn it, like a language,
and can't be dislodged thereafter.
In all your attractive worldliness, do you consider
the items crossed off the shopping list,
never to breathe again until the day
of bereavement stands open and naked like a woman

on a front porch, and do those you hobnob
with have any say or leverage in the matter?
Surely it feels like a child's feet propel us along

until everyone can explain.
Hell, it's only a ladder: structure
brought us here, and will be here when we're
honeycombs emptied of bees, and can say
That's all there is to say, babe, make it a good one
for me.

III

And when the hectic
light leaches upward into rolls of dark cloud
there will no longer be a contrast between thinking
and daily living. Light will be something even,
if remorseful, then. I say, swivel
your chair around, something cares, not the lamps
    purling
in the dark river, not the hot feet on the grass,
nor the cake emerging from the oven, nor the silver
trumpets on the sand: only a lining
that dictates the separation of this you from this some
    other,
and, in memorializing, drools. And if the hospice
gets over you this will be your magpie, this old hat,
when all is said, and done. No coffee, no rolls—
only a system of values, like the one printed
beside your height as it was measured as you grew
from child to urchin to young adult
and so on, back into the stitched wilderness
of sobs, sighs, songs, bells ringing, a thirst
for whatever could be discerned in the glacier—
tale, or tragedy, or talc—that backlit
these choices before we learned to talk
and so is a presence now, a posture like a chimney

that all men take to work with them
and that all see with our own eyes just
as the door is shutting, O shaft of light, O excellent,
   O irascible.

from *The New Yorker*

The Same Troubles with Beauty You've Always Had

◊　◊　◊

I still get the occasional snapshot in letters
crowded with bad news and rage and futile self-
aggrandizement, pictures of you in London or Belgium
or Corfu, depending on what man you're with taking you where,
or small-town modeling for hair salons or Florida
clothes stores, and I can see you're still someone whose
beauty is exercised like the bully on
the playground, to triumph in small, pointless ways,
and you've always been indisputably beautiful,
silencing every room you've ever walked into,
your lips pursed and carefully painted, your neck craned
upward in its fullest swannish arc. Apparently
you're having the same troubles with beauty you've always had,
men buying you plane tickets to Europe and after
a few weeks wishing you'd leave. How many strikes
have you taken, how many semi-rapes by boyfriends
with less patience for you than for the busy bartender?
How many times have you told me one of them had spread your legs
as you're sleeping, trying not to wake you?
How many abortions now? I remember the second,
which I drove you to, though it certainly wasn't my child,
and, with the clinic's appointments doubled up,
what should've taken hours took all day, every waiting seat
taken by the young girls and their mothers, their faces
like cliffsides, sitting silently in twos, each sinner

beside her own avenging angel. You even hushed them,
walking in like a diva to the cast party.
By never taking me to bed, you preserved me
for situations like this, the only friend you had left.
Every few hours I'd leave and call whom I was seeing then and
lie to her one of my famous white lies, told
with head held high, confident in its kindness.
Five hours later you were summoned, and I sat alone
with the two generations of women, reading
pamphlets. You stumbled coming out, and I drove you
not home, but to the empty house of your lover, a Turk
who claimed never to ejaculate and had his eye
on the 14-year-old boy next door. You sat on his couch
and cried, and I did what could be called my work or his,
I held you to my chest, to my heart. You've been thanking
me ever since, though the letters have trickled to maybe one
a year, and the photos you favor were taken years ago.
Unfocused that day, I remember the clinic
perhaps better than you, the thin, teary teenage girls
looking down at their laps unsure of what to fear more,
the surgery or their mothers, and hatred filling
the sometimes attractive, mothery faces
of the mothers like blood filling the nose of a drunk,
hatred for men, for children, for shame and weeping
and hatred, and as I watched all day long, each unfurled
old tissues from their sweater pockets and purses
and passed them with silent understanding to their children.

from *Ontario Review*

STEPHEN BERG

Cold Cash

◇ ◇ ◇

For Helen, at 60

O howls of crystal, milky souvenirs, desire piercing its own
   unsleeping eyeball with desire, glimpse of the ephemeral soul,
   bed where we talk and unfold and confess the impossibility of
   autobiography,

What else is there to our lives except your head raging with
   snakes and echoing skies, walls brushed gold by centuries of
   light, leisures of pure design, dreams of a relaxed god who
   serves and saves and provides whatever next wish blossoms
   into the faceless smile of mortality.

O birth of an endless self, imagine us without you, poor
   scavenging guests condemned to work, poor burgeoning
   weeds singing like poets without words,

Possibly value, possibly the last murder, possibly gray, possibly
   nothing less than a blind fuck in an alley, possibly tradition
   and belief, possibly even the wild god of hope inspiring the
   suicide of wishes, preventing our failure.

But imagine someone dying and you wake up and 18 million is
   yours, left by this unknown uncle from Davenport, Iowa, and
   there you are in the real world for once, not art, the world of
   having and owning and never having to die, of being better
   than, above, the world of gilded snot and full-fed lips and

sleep unbroken by loss, pigskin, peach silk cushions, cupolas, Louis XIV Roman chairs, the clear sweet light of complacency flowing in from Sardinia.

Who knows what it would mean, the central Chinese figure for this might be some wizened bald guy in robes sitting on a cushion chanting while I hum to myself "As Time Goes By," who knows what it is we really hope to achieve when one of those stark moments of truth overtakes us and we feel absolutely free, calm, happy even, and can choose anything instead of being held in suspense by all we know we can have,

Which is nothing according to Medusa's wailing mouth in the statue I saw reproduced in *House and Garden*, and tore out, and study right now as I am writing, thick gray slit of a mouth, huge voluptuous lips, blank eyes with a residue of carving where the pupils were done in relief, and of course snakes for hair.

And yet we think of love, and the failures and the relentless calling to us we hear from its pale villas and graves, war heroes, that's what lovers are, I can see us, the deepest glance into the soul, the gaze not even a high Mexican valley can equal.

The point is what can money do for us but remind our vulnerability to act and awaken to itself and become the new shield through which the army of nature with its loving unknown deaths may enter us and restore our souls to the laughter of revolving doors taking us from the inside weather of a lobby to the outside street of lighted buildings, skies, gusts of intense stupidity and fun.

So I was told by my real mother, whom I cannot remember, what could be crazier than to marry oneself but that's what money is, a broken egg at the bottom of a torn pocket, a tabletop in which we see our hungry faces, but there isn't a dish of anything on it for us to eat.

Very funny, someone cackles inside, I was only 5 when someone
handed me a book with ten red white and blue stamps in it
which would someday become a bond which would someday
become cash if I bought more stamps and waited long
enough, what was wrong with me? I just found that very
book in my dead mother's panty drawer, (I was collecting her
things), I guess I never cashed it in.

That's me, in my never-ending attempt to be a husband, not to
mention son, father, fisherman, gardener, runner, great lover,
just a normal American citizen, not Mayakovsky, not a guy
who believes he can face death without a tear or a little shit in
his pants,

And yet among these helpless ruminations there's another thing,
what does the earth want from us, if anything? what are we
supposed to do for the sake of it all as emissaries to an
unknown kingdom?

I thought this was funny once, but not now, not even the
weirdness of Mallarmé or a pheasant dinner can distract me
from asking how and why it was done, instead of answering
by picking out a Jaguar, Baum et Mercier, or a beachfront
condo to console my enviable loins.

O even my own ordinary tables and chairs are laughing at me
for having them so close, so deep in my mind that when I
come home nights I almost greet them with a word of praise
and relief, who belongs to whom? what a rich question, since
no more stories of the past are possible, on this yacht of
material possibility.

Sometimes in the bathroom I'll be standing there cock naked
loving every minute of it, maybe even liking that place and
time better than anything, the cozy steam of the hot water
turned on full, the mirror clouding up, readying myself with a
shave, then adjusting the shower water just right for the day
so I can step in under the stream and not decide how long to

take, feel I have hours, then begin to regret the necessary exit I'll be making before long into the dry commercial world of dog-eat-dog, of schedules and tasks, of making success better than that opposite term, which is, after all, the nature of the universe.

But will we ever know it, will the shower ever be our home? on certain days a feeling overtakes me, sits like a happy dog in my belly, of being poor, of having nothing but friends and poetry and a warm place to sleep, and it occurs to me that intelligence of this sort is denied to those who cannot hear the crystal howling or see the milky souvenirs or experience the despair of desire's baleful stare or know the soul's unyielding misery as it lies back letting its voice unfold the nonfactual snakes of light, of a destitute prompt unmotherly hammer driving in the nail, in the dirty unpainted wall of truth is beauty, beauty is truth, you know it and it's enough,

O which is why Let me touch you, Touch me, lie like two transparent knives willing to be picked up inside each of us, for no particular use, on no table, in no man's silver sheath, sparkling as the light at any time plays through their blades in the eternally joyful hands, ridiculous as Tolstoi, that cannot pick them up.

from *The Kenyon Review*

Interrogation

◇ ◇ ◇

When you have me as I'm standing
Against a wall, my sex becomes
Suddenly agnostic; strange new words
Slip out, your name mentioned twice.

This is not a careful time.
These bodies that have collected love,
That have closely followed the goals
Of line or curve, are becoming

Sentimental. We wander in and out
Of each other's mouths. I keep thinking
You're asking me something. Light
Pours in, hangs like a valuable stone above us.

I lose words remembering to speak.
You press into my skin for veins, finger
By finger, your eyes blank and glazed.
My eyes start to empty too, become

Exactly like yours, until all there is
Is a heart, each beat rendering the last silent.

from *Agni Review*

Chapter One

◊ ◊ ◊

We librarians went to Baja last weekend and sat in the sun
Ho! Ho! It's funny, isn't it? Though not really Henry Jamesian
It's not so simple that we're prim and went to the exotic
Though perhaps that's what the story really is.
We librarians went to Baja last weekend and sat in the sun
and walked on the beach and played tennis at the Head Clerk's club
Though we were vacationing without hierarchy.
In this way I love my job, bureaucrat that I am, I love
to rank, to answer, to box; I love the boolean in logic.
So perhaps that's why we went: Baja Mexico, if you've never been,
is about rusted cars growing into grass
on the side of the highway and shacks,
and roadside stands for olives and honey,
and Americans driving fast to the beach-and-tennis clubs they've built,
and the surfers in the ocean, waiting, rocking;
You see men standing in the no-man's land of the border,
waiting to cross: The border patrol jeeps with their rifles
ride by in the dust
Dirt roads and beer advertising everywhere
you look when you drive through Ensenada. We librarians
went to Baja last weekend and sat in the sun and we got a joke
    running:
what's the next fad in publishing after Co-Dependency?
It was a category of men who don't want to be success objects,
    we decided.
Self-help books for men who are eaten alive by women-mad-for-
    money.

You make them take a quiz, and everyone fits the category.
But my ex-boss, sitting there, and I are both in love with alcoholics,
She's married to hers and I've decided not to marry mine.
So maybe since we're prim and bookish we need the wild type—
I've thought about it. We laugh about these books
but just, just maybe. My ex-boss, now an administrator,
is the daughter of blacklisted Hollywood screenwriters.
She said they used to vacation right where we were when she was
   a kid.
They would dig for clams
in the bay that's going to be dredged into a marina for Americans.
Her family lived in exile, in Mexico.
She told me one day her husband doesn't believe those things
Really happened in America.
It's hard, though, to vacation without hierarchy.
Someone is the best tennis player, the best storyteller, the best
gossip, has the best body, gets along best. And you remember
where you stand as an employee. You remember
you're an American in a foreign country.
We librarians went to Baja and sat in the sun:
A day in the life, a *fete gallante*—
There was a house I wanted to run away from. Could I?

from *American Poetry Review*

Three Oranges

◊   ◊   ◊

first time my father overheard me listening to
this bit of music he asked me,
"what is it?"
"it's called Love for Three Oranges,"
I informed him.
"boy," he said, "that's getting it
cheap."
he meant sex.
listening to it
I always imagined three oranges
sitting there,
you know how orange they can
get,
so mightily orange.
maybe Prokofiev had meant
what my father
thought.
if so, I preferred it the
other way
the most horrible thing
I could think of
was part of me being
what ejaculated out of the
end of his
stupid penis.
I will never forgive him
for that,

his trick that I am stuck
with,
I find no nobility in
parenthood.
I say kill the Father
before he makes more
such as
I.

from *On The Bus*

At His Last Gig

◊　◊　◊

At his last gig in horrid Amsterdam—
City to which Camus consigned the fallen—
Ben Webster, Uncle Ben, then on the lam
From Denmark, escaping as always, swollen
And rheumy-eyed, spoke in a somewhat sullen
And more than somewhat smashed voice to the jam
Out front. It was his first speech, and a melan-
choly occasion. "You're growing and—" ham
That he was "—I'm going," he said. No scam,
However commonplace, wherever stolen;
He said it and he died, and no flim-flam.
But it *was* obnoxious. He was a felon,
　A brute, a drunk, a sob-sister. Yet song
　Was his in paradox his whole life long.

from *The Ohio Review*

TOM CLARK

Statue

◇ ◇ ◇

The angel asked, as his shoulders were pressed into the stone
Why me? And taken away from the inhabited body,
Like the lyric voice rustling from memory forests,
Childhood rushes toward death, a wind in those woods,
Crashing through trees, dying out,
Settling like a white mist over everything.

from *American Poetry Review*

"An Unlikely One Will Guide Me . . ."

◇   ◇   ◇

An unlikely one will guide me; I won't know I'm being helped. Will I know I am in trouble, that there's a distance to be crossed?

A fair life wouldn't tidy itself so well before its end.

I watch for the crone in the wood, helpful toad, cup of blood, distracted from peripheral magic. In my hasty desire I send away the boat which might carry me over.

But it's justice that the trickster slips every one of us a joke, the thing we live and die for. Serves us right and serves us well.

Who watches? Heroes are busy. Teachers are busy. Purpose is silent as ever, patient in folds of time.

If I came to the edge of my own, past streams of smoke and the noise of turbulence, handed-off delusion and want, then there would be no witness. Then I could let go of my precious heartache.

Burning cars, palms that itch, a brief flash beyond the hills. What I've learned has been added to me—superstition and dream as sure as numbers.

In the thick of uneasiness, a bit of the unreal peels away, leaves a new and pretty wound through to a timeless but ruffled spirit.

from Ploughshares

Sometimes in Winter

◇ ◇ ◇

I wonder whether
you've been avoiding
me purposely,
avoiding me
because you're afraid
that you do want me,
and fear that if
we met alone again,
we'd end up making love.

But maybe you avoid
me because you know
that I love you
and you don't love me,
and that's OK
if it's true—
or perhaps you avoid
me because you feel
that I'm already spoken for,
or you won't share
me with someone else.
It could be
that you don't want
to blot your notebook,
the one where you list
the things you believe in,
like Led Zeppelin,

Jesus Christ
and the importance of family.
Worst of all,
maybe you are in love
with that Virgo cop
who once complained
that your ice-cubes
had a sour odor.

Sometimes in winter
memory causes
a rose to bloom.
That's what happened
this morning as I walked
to the barbershop.
That rose remembered
Jeff Davis, someone
I went to college with.
He was born and raised
in Cortland, New York,
a town famous for its apples.
He was a few years older
than I was, and he had
a large following of friends
and acquaintances.
We both washed dishes
in the school cafeteria—
that's how we met.
When I moved out
of the dormitory,
I moved into a spare room
in his apartment.
He's the blueprint
for a major character
in my fiction—
it's through him
that I met the first
love of my life.

Well, Bernie calls
the other day
and reports
that Jeff was buried
in Cortland, a week ago
Sunday. Seems that somewhere
between six months
and three years ago,
Jeff contracted AIDS,
and believed that he
had been infected
by someone who knew
he was sick,
but who had sworn to him
that he was completely healthy.
When Jeff found out
that he had AIDS,
he stabbed the man
he thought had betrayed him,
to death. This seemed
impossible to me.
He spent some time in Riker's
but they released him
when it was apparent
that his life
was coming to an end.
Maybe he was
that skinny, homeless looking
guy who was walking
down Sixth Avenue
a few weeks ago
when I said to myself:
"NO! that can't be Jeff,
but it sure looks like him."

By then, war
had broken out
in the Persian Gulf.

I got in touch
with the first love
of my life,
(we hadn't spoken
in twenty years)
and gave her the bad news
about Jeff.
She had been his last
female lover.
It occurs to me
that I didn't intend
to write an elegy—
I wanted to celebrate today—
but death snuck right in here.

Sometimes in winter
you want to protect
all that you hold dear.
For now, summer is an impossible task,
and Sunday mornings will continue
to begin with Fauré's "Requiem."
Luckily, the students return on Monday.
Looking out the window
and seeing a fresh coat
of snow on the ground,
causes another rose to bloom—
the soldier who refuses to believe
that a soul can die,
or that you don't love him—
the one that remains
beautiful, unexplained.

from *Santa Monica Review*

Tuesday, June 4th, 1991

◊   ◊   ◊

By the time I get myself out of bed, my wife has left
the house to take her botany final and the painter
has arrived in his van and is already painting
the columns of the front porch white and the decking gray.

It is early June, a breezy and sun-riddled Tuesday
that would quickly be forgotten were it not for my
writing these few things down as I sit here empty-headed
at the typewriter with a cup of coffee, light and sweet.

I feel like the secretary to the morning whose only
responsibility is to take down its bright, airy dictation
until it's time to go to lunch with the other girls,
all of us ordering the cottage cheese with half a pear.

This is what stenographers do in courtrooms,
alert at their dark contraptions catching every word.
When there is a silence they sit still as I do, waiting
and listening, fingers resting lightly on the keys.

This is what Samuel Pepys did too, jotting down in
private ciphers minor events that would have otherwise
slipped into the heavy, amnesiac waters of the Thames.
His vigilance paid off finally when London caught fire

as mine does when the painter comes in for coffee
and says how much he likes this slow, vocal rendition
of "You Don't Know What Love Is" and I figure I will
make him a tape when he goes back to his brushes and pails.

Under the music I can hear the rush of cars and trucks
on the highway and every so often the new kitten, Felix,
hops into my lap and watches my fingers drumming out
a running record of this particular June Tuesday

as it unrolls before my eyes, a long intricate carpet
that I am walking on slowly with my head bowed
knowing that it is leading me to the quiet shrine
of the afternoon and the melancholy candles of evening.

If I look up, I see out the window the white stars
of clematis climbing a ladder of strings, a woodpile,
a stack of faded bricks, a small green garden of herbs,
things you would expect to find outside a window,

all written down now and placed in the setting
of a stanza as unalterably as they are seated
in their chairs in the ontological rooms of the world.
Yes, this is the kind of job I could succeed in,

an unpaid but contented amanuensis whose hands
are two birds fluttering on the lettered keys,
whose eyes see sunlight splashing through the leaves,
and the bright pink asterisks of honeysuckle

and the piano at the other end of this room with
its small vase of faded flowers and its empty bench.
So convinced am I that I have found my vocation,
tomorrow I will begin my chronicling earlier, at dawn,

a time when hangmen and farmers are up and doing,
when men holding pistols stand in a field back to back.
It is the time the ancients imagined in robes, as Eos
or Aurora, who would leave her sleeping husband in bed,

not to take her botany final, but to pull the sun,
her brother, over the horizon's brilliant rim,
her four-horse chariot aimed at the zenith of the sky.
But tomorrow, dawn will come the way I picture her,

barefoot and disheveled, standing outside my window
in one of the fragile cotton dresses of the poor.
She will look in at me with her thin arms extended,
offering a handful of birdsong and a small cup of light.

from *Poetry*

PETER COOLEY

Macular Degeneration

◊ ◊ ◊

Something like radiance is crossing my wife's face.
She won't admit it. I won't press her.
Now, while they happen, here are the facts:
my son is staring up into his mother's eyes;
we are standing in the kitchen at the day's beginning,
half-asleep over mugs of chicory swirling with cream;
he has just barreled in, five today, demanding
a cup of juice from her, not me. Not you,
he repeats. Of course, she fetches it, obedient.
Of course, I awakened the same slavery in my mother,
the need to be commanded by a man-child who is other,
forty years back. What boy could ask his father
with a glance to be maidservant and Queen of Heaven?
Tonight I will type my mother a short letter
since she has written me the facts about her vision—
that there is no cure for progressive scarring
of the retina from five years back and now she reads
slowly with a magnifying glass. I will detail
the feats of her grandson at his birthday party,
leaving out this morning's epiphany. Of course,
the instant he was born she could foresee this moment
because in her eyes he is her son, diminished,
and it is no one's business now how she relinquished me.

from *The Iowa Review*

litany

◇ ◇ ◇

Tom, will you let me love you in your restaurant?
i will let you make me a sandwich of your invention and i will
     eat it and call
it a carolyn sandwich. then you will kiss my lips and taste the
     mayonnaise and
that is how you shall love me in my restaurant

Tom, will you come to my empty beige apartment and help me
     set up my daybed?
yes, and i will put the screws in loosely so that when we move
     on it, later,
it will rock like a cradle and then you will know you are my
     baby

Tom, I am sitting on my dirt bike on the deck. Will you come
     out from the kitchen
and watch the people with me?
yes, and then we will race to your bedroom. i will win and we
     will tangle up
on your comforter while the sweat rains from our stomachs and
     foreheads

Tom, the stars are sitting in tonight like gumball gems in a little
     girl's
jewelry box. Later can we walk to the duck pond?

yes, and we can even go the long way past the jungle gym. i
        will push you on
the swing, but promise me you'll hold tight. if you fall i might
        disappear

Tom, can we make a baby together? I want to be a big pregnant
        woman with a
loved face and give you a squalling red daughter.
no, but i will come inside you and you will be my daughter

Tom, will you stay the night with me and sleep so close that we
        are one person?
no, but i will lay down on your sheets and taste you. there will
        be feathers
of you on my tongue and then i will never forget you

Tom, when we are in line at the convenience store can I put my
        hands in your
back pockets and my lips and nose in your baseball shirt and feel
        the crook
of your shoulder blade?
no, but later you can lay against me and almost touch me and
        when i go i will
leave my shirt for you to sleep in so that always at night you
        will be pressed
up against the thought of me

Tom, if I weep and want to wait until you need me will you
        promise that someday
you will need me?
no, but i will sit in silence while you rage, you can knock the
        chairs down
any mountain. i will always be the same and you will always
        wait

Tom, will you climb on top of the dumpster and steal the sun
        for me? It's just
hanging there and I want it.

no, it will burn my fingers. no one can have the sun: it's on loan
    from god.
but i will draw a picture of it and send it to you from richmond
    and then you
can smooth out the paper and you will have a piece of me as
    well as the sun

Tom, it's so hot here, and I think I'm being born. Will you
    come back from
Richmond and baptise me with sex and cool water?
i will come back from richmond. i will smooth the damp spiky
    hairs from the
back of your wet neck and then i will lick the salt off it. then i
    will leave

Tom, Richmond is so far away. How will I know how you love
    me?
i have left you. that is how you will know

from *American Poetry Review*

Repressed Theme

◊   ◊   ◊

But most of all my knowing I would write to her,
after sleeping through hours of broadcasting,
us backlit by so much moonlight and the population
            of the city immediately behind.

(Is it an idea to consider that the person
with whom one speaks less and less is the one
after all one came to see?)

The lightness I wake with—knowing *self*
as *fruit*; at bottom a pit unmarked
by sepulchral engravings—the ancient tombs at Tarquinia;
the body's weight in its perennial shift even as the sweetest
of savants rises upward in a tower of bells.

Is it our pet then, the hunchback who fondles
(even fucks) the gargoyle in the dream where
I wake to the pitch of your breaking voice?

Fragments, and only slender hope of offering
something more than obscure and less than obvious.
The instructions return cranked like a phonograph:

"Descend into the rooms of the ancient dead
who are by now non-existent against these lyrically
frescoed walls: a simple fish, a swallow, the horizontal
male figure suspended in the pastels of a pre-century century.

"Yes, open the tourist door to the armrail and stair,
a breath held 30 centuries exhumed in an era of nuclear silos
erect in a similar field. The absence of *them*, the absence
of their swords and lutes. A young girl's mirror surviving
like an accusation respecting you less and less for clinging
to a version wrought of things you cannot bear."

The exact position of the woman you love seated
for centuries in someone's arms by the fire.
The noon peach so juicy you have to lean over, it's painful.
This specter that rises like a scarecrow making visible
the acre in which it stands.

Orchards by sex to flesh from stones. This
body extended like a thought long believing
nothing after all is lost, not even by comparison.

from *Free Lunch*

The Window in Spring

◊   ◊   ◊

These weed-grown car hulks rusting in my neighbor's yard
Could be read as tokens of disdain for my neatness
Or as mere indifference to my feelings
If he weren't civil in other ways,
If he didn't take in my papers
When I go on vacation and forget to cancel.

When the eyesore rankles, I tell myself
He could be cooling his flesh with gloomy reminders
Like a hermit contemplating a skull
After the fall of Rome, killing off his hunger
For any abiding place on earth.

On my side of the fence, my garden
Already green, my apple trees and Japanese plums
Proclaim the triumph of husbandry
Dear to the yeomen of the republic,
Disciples of Jefferson.

I was the confident boy in grade school
Shouting the Pledge of Allegiance,
A natural patriot.
He may have been the nervous boy in back
Mouthing the words he couldn't feel,
Destined from the first to be a stranger.

Could be there's a cold mother behind him
Or an absent father, whose father in turn
Lost all he had in the Great Crash.

It's a free country when two perspectives like ours
Live side by side without rancor.
No one strolling our block can complain of boredom
Or a lack of options. Door-to-door salesmen
Won't prosper here unless they can vary their pitch,
Masters of many strategies, not merely one.

They tend to choose my house,
The house of a man who clearly cares about upkeep,
Gutters and siding, where my neighbor's junkyard
Seems, in its want of pretension,
Attractive to Witnesses for Jehovah,
Who come Sundays in pairs,
Bibles in hand, to fish for souls.

One of them could have been the girl in my grade school
Whose parents thought the Pledge a form of idolatry,
Who sat, hands folded tight, in silence.
If my parents had raised her, she'd be at home now
Weeding her flower garden or watching the news.

But here she is, or someone like her,
Venturing up my walk as the Bible commands.
She's going to ask what truth I rely on
To save the world, and what's my plan exactly
For convincing my neighbor he isn't stranded in Sodom
With no escape car while the streets are burning.

from *Shenandoah*

TIM DLUGOS

Healing the World from Battery Park

◊　◊　◊

> *Om Tara*
> *Tu Tara*
> *Ture Svaha*
> 　　—TIBETAN MANTRA

Draw a deep breath. Hold it. Let it go.
That's the smell of the ocean.
Our forebears hailed from out there. There's a stele
to mark the spot where Minuit exchanged
a mess of beads and trinkets for this island.
He may have thought it proof he was
a clever trader, although if the sky
were sky blue as today, the sunlight's flash
through bright glass would have been magnificent,
and that might have had tremendous value
in another culture. In another language,
"minuit" 's a division of the day.
I've divided my days among a host
of places near the sea. I get a lot
of comfort when I walk a beach, or through
the narrow streets among a crush of traders.
Sand in my shoes, sand of the Castle
Clinton courtyard where all of New York
turned out of yore to see the Jacksons,

Andrew and his wife. He'd whipped the bloody
British in the town of New Orleans
and massacred the Creeks. His steely eyes,
as blue as western skies, saw the space I see.
He breathed the same air. There's a little part
of him in me, that wants to drive away
the savages who populate the dark
expanse beyond the porch light's reach.
It takes a Trail of Tears to teach
that neighborhood improvement's not the point.
May the breath I draw become a balm
to soothe the exiled people of all times
and lands: the Cherokee, the Jew,
the people of Tibet whose loss brought us
abundant wisdom, the kulak and the Sioux,
the lover I abandoned and the friends
I drove away, the difficult and friendless
kicked out by their family, their school,
their church, their boss, their spouse, who found them too
impossible to put up with for one more minute.
In this park, their refuge, I divide my time
and feed it to the world when I exhale
like bread for ducks. It's not a fantasy
of power, and it's not about the rediscovery
of arcane treasure from a better place,
quieter and more romantic, like Tara
in the days of kings or in the antebellum
South. It's about the light that permeates
the sky above the boathouse where the sloop-
for-hire is moored. One romantic night,
it sailed across the harbor with my love
and me aboard. We drank champagne, and trailed
our fingers through the surface of the oil-
and-water stew that buoyed us. When we grew
apart, the two halves of a single wake
that break on banks across the dark expanse
of river from each other, I chose rage
to hold my sorrow's head beneath the waves

until I couldn't feel it anymore,
though somewhere under driftwood-littered slips
or in the trash-strewn slime a fathom down,
I knew that it was hiding. May the breath
I draw become a healing touch
to ease the pain I caused him, and to speed
the light that passed between and through us on
to its next stop. Here I divide my heart
among the teenaged couples and the shy
or clandestine romantics from the big
law firms who nuzzle on a bench, and queens
in stained Quiana shirts who cruise between
the slabs of stone with names of boys who died
in World War II. May it soothe my father,
who couldn't say how very much he loved
his wife, and all the tongue-tied men. And may
it heal the women, too; millions
like my mother who are left behind
when what they love about a man is wrenched
out of his body, hidden in another place.
In another language, "Tara" is the name
of a she-god sprung out of a human tear.
She heals all wounds and brings the world a sense
of peace. On this island where the gods
would outnumber the humans in a week if such
a mode of birth became habitual,
I beg her presence as I feel my breath
flying like a jet from Newark
out into the world. There's a quantity
of tenderness I feel sometimes
that drops into my chest precipitous
and golden as the sun into Fort Lee.
I couldn't tell you where it comes from, but
I'm learning where it hides. It's in the nectarine
you ate for breakfast, or the thing
you're doing now, not in what you think
you should do or in what comes next.
And it's not in what you think "God" means;

the only certainty is that you're wrong.
Draw a deep breath. Thank you, mother.
Hold the light inside and let it find
the ragged spots, a gentle tongue to probe
for caries. Then expire.
A little part of you is in the wind now,
a trace of pain or coffee in the scent
of brine that clasps you like a lover,
closer and more faithful than a lover.
Bless me, father. This is my first
confession: I'm living in the light
at the bottom of a sea of air,
everything I need in a place I share
with everyone. It's in your hands.

from *Hanging Loose*

Favorite Iraqi Soldier

◇   ◇   ◇

Into his kit when sent to the front he had tucked
his black three-piece suit and through night
after night of the frightful bombing, which
not only wiped out but pragmatically entombed

his luckless comrades in a marvel of technological
decadence, he had kept the suit protected
so that at the surrender he had stripped naked
and slipped it on. This is when the photographer

caught him, that among the thousands of defeated
there walked one Iraqi in a three-piece suit
who tried to express by his general indifference
that he had stumbled into all this carnage simply

by accident and was now intent on strolling away.
I am a modest banker tossed on the wrong bus.
I am a humble stockbroker who took a wrong turn.
And he passed through the American lines

and began hitchhiking south. Did he elect
to relocate in Kuwait? Fat chance! Did he
want the lovable Saudis as new neighbors?
Quite unlikely! What about the opportunities

offered by the Libyans, Tunisians, Egyptians?
Truly hilarious! Was there any place in Africa
where he hoped to lay his head? Decidedly
not! What about Europe where he could start

as a servant or chop vegetables in the back
of a restaurant but work his way up? Completely
crazy! Or North America where he could dig
a ditch but with the right breaks might buy

a used car? Too ludicrous! What about South
America where he could pick fruit or Asia where
he could toil in a sweatshop? You must be nuts!
In his black suit he is already dressed for the part

and hopes to hitchhike to one of those Antarctic
islands and stroll around with the penguins.
Good evening Mr. White, good evening Mrs. Black,
your children swim quite nicely, they look

so hardy and fit. No one to give him orders
but the weather. No one to terrify him
but the occasional shark. No one to be mean to
but the little fish, who were put into this ocean

to serve him and who he praises with each bite.
Thank you, gray brother, for the honor you have bestowed
on my belly. May you have the opportunity
to devour me when my days on earth are done.

from *The Paris Review*

Feminism

◇   ◇   ◇

All over the world, Little Bees, Star Scouts,
and Blue Birds play Telephone, whispering messages
in a chain link of ears—no repeating (that's cheating),
only relaying what they hear their first shot.
Sometimes "Molly Loves Billy" becomes "A Holiday in Fiji,"
or "Do the Right Thing" becomes "The Man Who Would Be King."
Still, there is trust. Girls taking the Blind Walk,
a bandanna around one's eyes (Pin the Tail on the Donkey-style)
as another leads her through the woods
or a backyard or entire city blocks. Girls helping
where they are needed or inventing ways to aid
where they seemingly are not. Memorizing remedies
for cuts and stings, frostbite, nosebleeds.
Their motto: Be prepared at all times.
Full of anxiety, they watch for home hazards,
check for frayed toaster or hair dryer cords.
Outside, they watch for color changes in cloud formations,
the darkening of the sky. They're safest in cars
during electrical storms.
                          There's so much to remember and learn.
So many impending disasters, yet so many well wishes
for their world. These girls shut the tap
as they brush their teeth, secure glow-in-the-dark reflectors
on their bikes, and do at least one good turn daily.
They are taught that alone they are small,
but if they can empathize with each other, they can gain power.
Just to see what it feels like, a walking girl

may spend an afternoon in a wheelchair. Another
may stuff cotton in her ears. And to be readied
for what lies ahead when they grow up
and they're no longer Girl Scouts, they make collages
cutting images from magazines showing what they might be:
mothers or lawyers, reporters or nurses.
Or they play Rabbit Without A House, a Brazilian form
of London Bridge, or American Musical Chairs.
There will always be an odd number of girls, always
one left out. The earth and her scarce resources.
Survival in Sudan begins with Sheep and Hyena.
And though all the girls may try to protect the one
who is the Sheep in the middle of their circle, most often
the outside Hyena does not give up
and breaks through sore forearms and weakened wrists
to eat her. Red Rover, Red Rover,
it is better when Girl Scouts stay together.
So they bond tightly in their Human Knot,
a female version of a football team's huddle.
And all holding hands, they squeeze their Friendship Squeeze,
knowing each small one-at-a-time grip
is like a Christmas tree light, each a twinkle
the rest of the strand cannot do without.
Each missing face on the missing child poster
like the fairest of all looking into her mirror.

from *Hanging Loose*

STEPHEN DUNN

The Vanishings

◇ ◇ ◇

One day it will vanish,
how you felt when you were overwhelmed
by her, soaping each other in the shower,
or when you heard the news
of his death, there in the T-Bone diner
on Queens Boulevard amid the shouts
of short-order cooks, Armenian, oblivious.
One day one thing and then a dear other
will blur and though they won't be lost
they won't mean as much,
that motorcycle ride on the dirt road
to the deserted beach near Cadiz,
the Guardia mistaking you for a drug-runner,
his machine gun in your belly—
already history now, merely *your* history,
which means everything to you.
You strain to bring back
your mother's full face and full body
before her illness, the arc and tenor
of family dinners, the mysteries
of radio, and Charlie Collins,
eight years old, inviting you
to his house to see the largest turd
that had ever come from him, unflushed.
One day there'll be almost nothing
except what you've written down,
then only what you've written down well,

then little of that.
The march on Washington in '68
where you hoped to change the world
and meet beautiful, sensitive women
is choreography now, cops on horses,
everyone backing off, stepping forward.
The exam you stole and put back unseen
has become one of your stories,
overtold, tainted with charm.
All of it, anyway, will go the way of icebergs
come summer, the small chunks floating
in the Adriatic until they're only water,
pure, and someone taking sad pride
that he can swim in it, numbly.
For you, though, loss, almost painless,
that Senior Prom at the Latin Quarter—
Count Basie and Sarah Vaughan, and you
just interested in your date's cleavage
and staying out all night at Jones Beach,
the small dune fires fueled by driftwood.
You can't remember a riff or a song,
and your date's a woman now, married,
has had sex as you have
some few thousand times, good sex
and forgettable sex, even boring sex,
oh you never could have imagined
back then with the waves crashing
what the body could erase.
It's vanishing as you speak, the soul-grit,
the story-fodder,
everything you retrieve is your past,
everything you let go
goes to memory's out-box, open on all sides,
in cahoots with thin air.
The jobs you didn't get vanish like scabs.
Her good-bye, causing the phone to slip
from your hand, doesn't hurt anymore,
too much doesn't hurt anymore,

not even that hint of your father, ghost-thumping
on your roof in Spain, hurts anymore.
You understand and therefore hate
because you hate the passivity of understanding
that your worst rage and finest
private gesture will flatten and collapse
into history, become invisible
like defeats inside houses. Then something happens
(it is happening) which won't vanish fast enough,
your voice fails, chokes to silence;
hurt (how could you have forgotten?) hurts.
Every other truth in the world, out of respect,
slides over, makes room for its superior.

from *The Paris Review*

Shoelace

◇ ◇ ◇

Her deceased husband's shoelace must be unknotted;
the widow, plunging her face at the foot of the casket,
sets her teeth to work. Little changes: long ago
some villages believed the soul would fret with such a knot
and thus be kept from its journey, whereas others (spooked
about sundown) used to drape fishnets over their dead
to keep them from rising up and roving as vampires.
As for the widow—whose folklore flickers, thoughts

consisting of non sequiturs—she can scarcely focus
on her fingernails loosening the knot; the rest of her
feels floaty, awobble as someone trying to stand up
in a rowboat. Now she knows: we live above a gulf
from which, fog-huge, rise nightmares (disease, car wrecks,
endlessly) that snuff the luminous flesh we love.
She ties his shoelace. Our dopey hope and deep deep
need for ceremony show in that neat black bow.

from *Phoebe*

The Necessity

◇ ◇ ◇

It isn't true about the lambs.
They are not meek.
They are curious and wild,
full of the passion of spring.
They are lovable,
and they are not silent when hungry.

Tonight the last of the triplet lambs
is piercing the quiet with its need.
Its siblings are stronger
and will not let it eat.

I am its keeper, the farmer, its mother.
I will go down to it in the dark,
in the cold barn,
and hold it in my arms.

But it will not lie still—it is not meek.

I will stand in the open doorway
under the weight of watching trees and moon,
and care for it as one of my own.

But it will not love me—it is not meek.

Drink, little one. Take what I can give you.
Tonight the whole world prowls
the perimeters of your life.

Your anger keeps you alive—
it's your only chance.
So I know what I must do
after I have fed you.

I will shape my mouth to the shape
of the sharpest words—
even those bred in silence.

I will impale with words every ear
pressed upon open air.
I will not be meek.

You remind me of the necessity
of having more hope than fear,
and of sounding out terrible names.

I am to cry out loud
like a hungry lamb, cry loud
enough to waken wolves in the night.

No one can be allowed to sleep.

from *Boston Review*

One Kiss

◇   ◇   ◇

A man was given one kiss, one
mouth, one tongue, one early dawn, one boat
on the sea, lust of an indeterminate
amount under stars. He was happy
and well fitted for life until he met a man
with two cocks. Then a sense of futility
and of the great unfairness of life befell him.
He lay about all day like a teenaged girl dreaming,
practicing all the ways to be unconsciously beautiful.

Gradually his competitive spirit began to fade
and in its place a gigantic kiss rowed toward him.
It seemed to recognize him, to have intended itself
only for him. It's just a kiss, he thought,
I'll use it up. The kiss had the same thing
on its mind—"I'll use up this man."

But when two kisses kiss, it's like tigers
answering questions about infinity with their teeth.
Even if you are eaten, it's okay—you just become impossible
a new way—sleepless, stranger than fish, stranger
than some goofy man with two cocks. That's
what I meant about the hazards

of infinity. When you at last begin to seize those things
which don't exist,
how much longer will the night need to be?

from *Fine Madness*

Life Is Happy,

◊   ◊   ◊

I suddenly understand: I'm watching you chop away
at a cabbage, you're humming, the kitchen is light
and knife-thrust, light and knife-thrust,
lightslaw, airslaw, and humming. That would be the way
Life gets its blade out, then goes at it
with a human heart: maybe like somebody hacking
jungle undergrowth, so the whole heart's lost in a minute,
ribbons, pulp; or maybe making an exquisite show
of almondlike slivers, holding up
the fussy ricegrain-sized inscribings, studying
its artistry from many angles, taking years,
taking seventy years; but humming
in an absentminded, pleasurable way, no matter
the time involved, or what the technique—happy. This
was the lesson, now I remember, carried by the moted light
of the bulky, asthmatically-purring projector
they used for grade school "nature films." The room
was darkened, our tittering hushed, and then a voice,
a grave yet understanding, deeply male voice, came forth
from that machine, while on the screen a grainy lion
brought a grainy zebra down, and this was followed
by a few frames of its running with the bowel. This
was "the law of the jungle," "the law of fang and claw," and
so we understood that what we saw
as horrifying slaughter—and that zebra's widened jaws
and splayed gray teeth would bray inside my brain
for years—was part of a governing system, a balance:

there was pain, but it was ordered pain, and Life
was in the greenish jungle vapor, or the sky, all the while,
surveying its handiwork, calmly. Not *a life*, but Life
was happy, standing grandly in the kitchen
with its tools and its purview, neither king nor cabbage
more endeared to it, the knife out, at some moments
even looking like love, its hair, its hips,
its smooth, assumed efficiency,
its dearly off-key humming.

from *Boulevard*

What the Instant Contains

◊ ◊ ◊

(Lyle Van Waning, 1922–1988)

Presently Lyle gets into bed.
The amaryllis on the sill hum.
The dust starts inventing the afterwards.
He is not getting up again.

The dust starts inventing the afterwards.
The whole thing from the ground up.
The *presently.* The *Lyle gets into bed.*
The amaryllis on the sill hum.

The roses on the wall grow virulent.
Then dreadful in increasing dimness.
Then even the wicked no longer matter.
Even the one who would steal the water of life goes under,

even the unread last 49 pages
of the mystery novel on the kitchen table,
(the sill under the amaryllis hums),
even the ancient family name,

even the woman he never found.
If you sit there, near him, in the sofa chair,
if you look at him and he's sleeping now, curled,
the oxygen furious in its blank tubes,

you can hear the wind as it touches the panes,
then, as the wind drops, bushtips brushing the panes,
buds on the tips,
then, as the wind stills altogether,

the weight of the air on the panes,
the face of the air not moving,
the time of day adhering to the panes,
the density of the light where the glass fits the frame

of the windows Lyle built
in the walls Lyle built,
all of it adhering—glass to light, light to time—
all of it unable to advance any further,

here now, arrived. If you sit here,
if you sit in your attention watching him sleep,
if it is still sleep,
looking past the vials and the industrial oxygen tanks,

hearing the tap at the pane,
hearing the tap, click, as the wildgrasses rap
as the wind picks up,

looking into his closed face for the gaze,

you will see, if you can posit the stillness
that beats on its pendulum at the heart of the room,
x beats per minute,
if you can place it at the center,

the beat of the stillness swinging on its tiny firm arc,
like a face on a string, perfect, back and forth,
to permit the center of the center to glow,
you will see the distance start to grow

on the shore of the endlessly lain-down face,
yellow shore which the wide hand holds—
right there on the pinpoint of the face in the room . . .

When he wakes I will give him some water.
I will try to feed him some soup.
We will try to drive back into the body
what roves around it,

will try to darken the body with a red flush,
make it affirm itself in relation to the light again,
make it *know* something, make it grow dull again,
instead of this translucence, this mirror becoming glass,

dents in it, sockets, tape on the left cheek
pulling the papery skinfolds back
to hold the nostril open
to fit the radiant tube inside.

But now the face is going faster, faster

—*floor sills dust* going the other way,
the whole marriage pulling apart—his dream from the drawer,
waiting from skin—
Now he opens his eyes and looks across *the room* at me,

now there are men on the bed with him, many men, naked,

one puts his fist in another's mouth,
one puts his fingers in another's ears,
another's fingers are in there now too,

they put their hands on each other's feet, they roil,
there's a shield in the air but you cannot see it,
it's the thing the dust makes when it's cast up,
there are elements from *history*,

the air hums, edges, undersides, bevelled lips,
shadows behind the edges, ears, fingers,
Circe there on her throne in her shining robe
with golden mantle and the place was lovely

and nymphs and naiads waiting on her
carding no fleece, spinning no wool, but only
sorting, arranging from confusion
in separate baskets the bright-colored flowers,

the different herbs,
and where we had shoulders we have no shoulders
and where our arms were in their right places
there are no arms, there are no right places,

her song would move the wood, would stop the
streams, would stay the wandering birds,
her song would move the wood
would stop the stream

would stay the wandering *afterwards*. Tap tap.
Presently the cast-iron stove,
with metal fruit upon its wondrous flanks, is cold,
grapes swelling there, and apples, pears.

I put my hand on them.
I press my palm onto the icy fruit.
Tap tap the flowertips.
The heart of waiting. Tap.

There are two directions—fast—in the instant,
two, tangled up into each other, blurred, bled,
two motions in every stillness,
to make a body, a waiting—

the motion into here, the firming up,
chest paper book face leaf branch drawer,

the order of events, days, days,

something like a head at the top, stiff,
the minutes flowing off into limbs, fingertips,
the trunk made of actions-that-can't-be-undone,
shield high,

the first minute of existence ruffling like feathers or hair
at the top of his crown, stilling,
the next minute arriving, stilling,
all of him standing there on his crucial deeds, on the out-

come, growing ever more still.
And then, faster and faster—the other direction: *her,*
the silvery thing which is the absence of properties,
the enchantment of itself with itself whirling,

both itself and the hole it leaves—fed by dream—
fed by each glance in the mirror however swift in passing,
moving suddenly in limbs that are not limbs,
moving with a will not yet an individual will—

and the room containing this flow or being contained
                                            by it,
and Lyle momentarily on the crest till the wave breaks again,

and Lyle being distributed partly to him partly to her,
torn up and thrust,
(I want to forget it, I want to forget what I saw),
the face riding for a moment longer on the spray,

the *look* on the face riding after the face has
                              dissolved,
for just a moment longer the gaze in the eye looking out,
                                        tossed out—

dust lifting and drifting—
specks and sparkles of dust in the empty room—
then us walking by a mirror on our way out and looking in,
and us being fooled for a moment longer

before we realize what's in there, look,
does not belong to us at all
but is an argument tossed out
                                    in that instant
for the sake of discussion

by the queen on the other side
on her throne with shining robes and golden mantle
(and the place lovely)
towards him whom she loves

to convince him, to undo him.
I look in there at it a moment longer—my face—my
expression—
flung out into the room by her for the sake of discussion—

the features on there a phrase—not even—the lilt in, the

intonation of, a phrase, brisk, a tactic, quick,
from her in the room where the cloth is not woven
only colors sorted back into that separateness

the earth in its fields has momentarily blurred—
columbine, fire-on-the-mountain, vetch and iris—
                                                    the iris
so early this year as we leave, and waving in patches of sun—

and then the blue vase I'll put them in for a time.

from *Epoch*

Great Work Farm Elegy

◇ ◇ ◇

1.

In Adam's house, in Paradise, the room is still.
The hours, equal. The windows, open to the air.
The floor is swept. The flowers, real. The light
Is far *and* near—like water, very very clear
As it was in the beginning of the hours:
Before the bay of the world did empty out
Its light into the sea of light. And from the shore
The sea withdrew afar, and gathered up, and towered;
And night descended gradual and great with all its fires,
And at the door pale death knocked with his foot . . .

2.

All night, seated beneath the willows you know of,
On every watermeadow of the universe, we write
The long letters of mind by the light of the moon.
But now day breaks, and a million suns say:
"*Send it!*"—And I (for one) reply: "To whom?
To the townsfolk of New Ulm? Or the great Bog of Cloon?"
"No!" says the one sun that sees me. "Send it
To your own whom you dare not name! To her,
The loon on the lake; to him, at the shore: the countenance
In the abyss—with copies to your death, etc."

Why not say it? You blue-eyed infant souls!
I am here to tell you on this shaken earth:
Our face, and the form of our bodies, are not
Known to us. And the elevation of the golden house
We build is unknown to us. And the gods of the house,
That stand inside, are, as I have said elsewhere,
Enraged. Judgement has not yet been passed, nor
The sentence written, nor the harvest carried home:
But the fields are white with the risen grain.
And the witnesses clamor in the porch and on the stair

4.

And crowd the threshold, where they pause—some still
In the open air, under the raking light,
Their harbinger that chalks the door. Is it
A dream, householders? Oh no! The children have
Come home out of the air, like rain or snow . . .
For what, then, do we build this house and keep it
But for the children?—Now, as at all times,
I hear them. *Now*, I see their painted clothes.
And the room darkens and ignites, as the clouds
Slake and re-illume the low sun of the dawn.

5.

One says, "Old man! You lectured in my dreams,
And uttered words I did not understand. *Either*
You did not speak clearly, as often you do not;
Or I did not pay attention. (Often I don't.) So!
We have come to give you *another chance*. Explain
Again what you said in my dream. What did you
Say? What did you *mean*? What!"—Now, more than ever,

I hear them at my door, laughing and talking
Among themselves, and putting their question
Under the raking light, on the shore of the sky.

6.

—*I will explain*: "The earth is mourning ('*Toha!*')
And crying ('*Boha!*'), because her lot is evil."
"Know this!" (I say) "The earth is broken, creased,
Scratched, crazed, pitted, torn, always in motion,
Ribbed, rock-ribbed, wrinkled as the skin of
A starving animal and scarred—or radiant
Like the body of a woman who arose to bathe,
And then lay down again to rest and consider.
And the air is never still for all the vows
('Love of my life,' etc.), and the switching of engines.

7.

"And I make no difference for mind, that 'ocean.'
What, then, does it mean to begin again, *dilectissimi*,
As if from the beginning? It means just this:
To be penetrated by a dark myth—in order
To leave it empty at your death, like a book
Forgotten on the asphalt that becomes, thereby,
The one dark book which makes good sense. The wind
Opens it. And the rains of a long summer
Evening erase the pages, and the very page.
And there it lies, a ruin. And is never found.

8.

"And the woman says—the one, you will remember,
Who lay down again to consider: 'The light
Has betrayed me, the low light of the dawn.'

'Darken the room,' she says. 'Write me no more letters,
Under the willows by the light of the moon.'
—So I tell her the story of the great work
In the beginning: How under the willows
On all the watermeadows of the universe
Our hand began the long letters of mind
For her, with copies to our death, etc. . . .

9.

" 'Then as now' (I say) 'the Rider was on high,
Killing and quickening, as it is written,
Sowing and reaping, and feeding the rain
That rots the stack.' " ("What!" the children cry. "Say
What?" "Look up!" is my reply. "It's clear as day,
Dilectissimi.")—"There was a farmer, Herman;
His wife, Irene; and I was the boy. Late summer.
The bales lay in the field. And time that is
Destroying me appeared to me in the low light,
Awaking the thirty dogs of the farm

10.

"(Old and young, lame skeletons and firm-fleshed,
Farting hounds) to the hunt that followed on
Among the bales, across the stubble fields
Of timothy (a grass that loves the marshes,
A running root), behind the Rider of the sky,
Gigantic form. The earth, with all its scars,
Lay open to the eye—the harvest of the hay.
And a cloud that shone like a hammered rail
Overhung the river, far to the north,
Toward which the farmer drove us in his Plymouth

11.

"Automobile—like a bat out of hell.
In the neighbor farm, at the river's edge,
A birthday was going on—an overheated
Kitchen, strange animals, and the *Weiberdeutch*
(Dreary language of carnal origin),
The wisdom of the women of New Ulm.
And strange! Strange to tell! Over the lawn, I saw
A white moon, and the moon's shine, bright and thin.
From the river came a dreadful storm.
'A prodigy!' sang the women of New Ulm.

12.

"—'The hay,' the farmer whispered. 'The hay will come
To harm'. Then back we went, from north to south,
Returning home at noon, like a whizzing bat,
In the Plymouth ('38) which he drove flat out.
Such was the beginning of the great work
And the dark myth (of which I spoke)—the lost
Book the wind opens, and the rains of long summer
Evenings, pouring down, erase: all the pages,
And the very page (as the heart of a man
Is emptied at the moment of his death);

13.

"And it becomes—the very page—a memory
Of memories to be, or not to be,
Remembered; and of the dreams of love unknown,
The dream. And of the work without a name,
In a nation undiscovered and its wars,
The distant glory and the murmured fame.
Thus begins, *dilectissimi,* the extreme

Poem of the wind and rain, long letter of mind
Addressed to the abyss—*and sent*: how it was
When there were two of us on earth alone,

14.

"A man, a boy, and a thousand bales of timothy
(A grass that loves old pastures, a running root
Knotted in wires by machines)—each 90
Pounds for sure, or more when it's wet . . . .
—The Rider of the sky led on the hunt
Followed by the thirty storm hounds of the *Great
Work Farm*, each dog with its note, each under each
Intent upon his lesson:—like didactic angels
Out of the fountains of Maimonides,
Each hound with its own harsh bell. From noon

15.

"Until the afternoon, from afternoon until
The dark the farmer of earth threw up a thousand
Bails of timothy onto the rig. I drove;
And from the rick, allegory of the work,
We built—Herman and I—the golden house
Of the stack that kept the hay from harm.
All day above our heads the Rider of the sky
Pursued the Scorpion, the Bison, and the Dragon Fly
Until the hay was in and the rain came down.
Then the thirty hounds of the farm (in chorus) sang

16.

" 'The Song of the Constant Nymph,' and the heavens rang:
'Which are the hours of greatest simplicity?
Are they among the hours of the day:

The morning hours, for example, witness of children
In the raking light? Or are they the hours of the sun
At noon, a little before, or a little after,
The meridian which says, 'Behold! The general meadow!'
Or are they among the evening hours, crepuscular,
That await pale death, the guest with the swift kick,
The same at every door.—Which are the hours

17.

" 'Of greatest simplicity? Are they among
The first watches of the night, the teaching powers,
When the tides of light withdraw from shore—far off,
Far out—and from the distant beacons and the towers
Difference and the dark, histories of light,
Instruct the heart.—Which are the hours of greatest
Simplicity? Are they planted among the midnight
Hours when the earth stands like a statue in
The general meadow—a statue in winter
Like a woman in time without a sister

18.

" 'Who has stopped for a moment on a winter hill,
Without past or future, the same in every season,
Dark Niobe of the lovely lovely tresses,
Without a reason.—Which are the hours of
The greatest simplicity? Are they, perhaps, among
The darkest hours of the night when the monks
Begin their chant: "Or has the sight of the sun
In its glory," they sing, "Or the glow of the moon
As it walks the sky, secretly stolen my heart
Away so that I blew them a kiss . . . ?" '

19.

"Then the Rider of the sky—the master of
The Scorpion, and the Dragon Fly—answered his hounds
And sang this conclusion: 'These are the hours
Of greatest simplicity: *the hours before dawn*—
When the earth has risen from consideration
After her bath, and walks abroad alone
Conferring honor where it's due—among
The sleeping flowers in the garden. And the children
In their painted clothes, living and dead,
Crowd the doorway (the dead ones are in blue)

20.

" 'Putting their questions. "All honor," says the earth
"To our brightest flower, the noblest of the family,
The one who knew the work—and now stands here
(*Toha*) in blue." "Who is the rider of the sky?",
The dead one asks. "*Who is that masked man?*"—"I am
The truth of the messenger" (was his reply),
"Not this word or that one ('long letters of mind'),
But a short scroll under the tongue signifying
The whole breath: past, passing, and to come . . .
—And I am of water the iron fountain,

21.

" '*Dilectissimi*, which explodes at the punctual
Moment of any dawn, multiplying the sun;
And the water, overflowing from that hour
Into the gravity and then the grave of time,
Becomes our truth . . . this lovely one.
—And I am the dark myth emptied at your death,
Dilectissimi, which other children find

On rainy evenings: an object lesson to
Keep them kind, like the gallows and the gibbet
And the executioner—good at ending.' "

from *Colorado Review*

The Butcher's Son

◇   ◇   ◇

Mr. Pierce the butcher
Got news his son was missing
About a month before
The closing of the war.
A bald man, tall and careful,
He stood in his shop and found
No bottom to his sadness,
Nowhere for it to stop.
When my aunt came through the door,
Delivering the milk,
He spoke, with his quiet air
Of a considerate teacher,
But words weren't up to it;
He turned back to the meat.

The message was in error.
Later that humid summer,
At a local high-school fête,
I saw, returned, the son
Still in his uniform.
Mr. Pierce was not there
But was as if implied
In the son who looked like him,
Except he had red hair.
For I recall him well,
Encircled by his friends,
Beaming a life charged now

Doubly because restored,
And recall also how
Within his hearty smile
His lips contained his father's,
Like a light within the light
That he turned everywhere.

from *The New Yorker*

DONALD HALL

Pluvia

◇　◇　◇

In the nation of rainy days
    tractor-trailers spray and glissade
gray through rain down blacktop
    with a sound like cloth tearing;
an airplane circles above clouds
    that conceal the balding mountain
and engine-sounds waver like a dream
    voice saying, "please, please."

In the nation of rainy days
    the white cottage downstreet vanishes
into gray air, disappearing
    like a vessel lost in a hurricane;
rain draws wavery vertical lines
    against the black doors of a barn
and chimneysmoke kneels on flattened
    grass, praying to dissipate.

In the nation of rainy days
    clouds hang tatters of shaggy muslin
as pale as winter on maples
    that sink like shipwrecked cottages;
deer lost in overgrown orchards
    dissolve in the mist and drizzle;
abandoned by honeybees, old roses
    and soaked clover curve earthward.

Day after day, we wake to green rain
    drenching the garden; we slog
through our chores slow-dancing
    to rain's brute tune that drones
the same saturated phrase in the same
    cadence again and again
like a lost airplane still circling
    over the nation of rainy days.

from *The Nation*

Vegetable Wisdom

◇   ◇   ◇

You want to tell me how it seemed
the day you fell in love at the Blue Parrot
and the night in Washington Square when you felt
a weird hitherto undescribed floating absence of love
and how much it hurt that day on Waterman Street
across from Faunce House when the cars passing
were just clots of metal and the poetry books
were just wads of flattened wood because
Cathleen had walked away . . . .
You want to spill those old dark beans.
They seem to choke you. They threaten to burst
with undigested meaning—

but why does it have to be me, a total stranger
who has to listen and soak it all up?
Your trust in me is a strange miscalculation;
you seem to believe I'm a future lover or brother
whose heart holds a certain space waiting to be filled
precisely by how you feel about how you felt
in Dilemma XY or Situation Q.
No, baby. You have the wrong number,
you were sold some bad information; I am someone
quite other. To me
the exact shading of how your mother in her gold bathrobe
suffered through her final months
(as perceived by you)
and how your father was brave in the silence of the kitchen

(as perceived by you)
is only distantly of interest like bright clothing
that flaps on a line behind some humble dwelling
seen from a fast bus. You see what I'm saying?
I'm a kind of receiver who can take your jewels of memory
and call them beans, beans you want to throw up.
It's a dubious metaphor but I don't really care
the way you in your bean-puffed pride feel sure
I must care—I am something *else*, you sensitive drip!
You're so pitifully pleased to address a total stranger
but that's because you have no idea how totally I am
a stranger. Will you take some advice from a stranger?
Put that poem back in your fat little filing cabinet.
And then what? Then what? Then try to be strong:
like a plant, a bush, a tree;
a tree's nobility is poemless.
My own agenda is to grow and fulfill myself
without bothering anybody else, under the stars, under the
    sun,
with the wind in my hair, smelling the salt sea breeze,
hearing the indecipherable songs of birds
and the alien croaking of frogs content to be frogs.
One zucchini does not ask another zucchini for praise.

from *Virginia Quarterly Review*

Argument

◇   ◇   ◇

But it ate a hole in my heart,
she said when I complimented her
on the use of restraint, so useful
in the ongoingness of shared life,
life at the midpoint, where we are.

We note how even the offspring of friends
frankly worry about their own aging.
We note the second generation
of pets, whose kidneys have already
begun to fail, their balance fading,

giving up the body's tension.
What did I say to establish
that tension in our bodies?
Did she just give in for the sake
of a good night's sleep, nothing countered

to keep us up and at it, to turn
over what's been tossed often enough?
Her fair head's an aquarium
of trouble, troubling through troubled sleep.
The cost? One more entry through the heart.

from *Western Humanities Review*

Theory

◇ ◇ ◇

X could make a face like a fish.
Standing on the sidewalk,
he threw underwater kisses
at a store window where he saw himself.
Someone thought he was crazy.
But X had a theory that had to do
with memory, change, music, and danger.
Everything he remembered
turned purple in his mind,
or it remained this dead white thing
he'd want to shake out of his head.
Plus there was always a difference
between what was and is,
a sad gap like a pause in a song.
Everything converted to fiction
because of the passage of time,
mythless histories that bent in the telling,
like pencils placed in glasses of water.
Since knowing himself
required a marginal reading
too distant for eloquence,
too intimate for communion,
he was always, in theory, something else.
This made beautiful sense.
And yet there was a terror of being
neither person, dream, nor language.
He was, in a sense, a story of his

own invention, except without design.
Each step across a room
required a degree of calculation,
like a painter doing self-portraits
who erases the face each morning.
"Inexact but precise"
in his rendering of life,
X saw a fish with tinfoil eyes
drowning in light outside a hardware store.
This was only a theory and yet
what is a stone but a theory of change?

from *Ploughshares*

DAVID IGNATOW

Absolutely

◇   ◇   ◇

Now the idea is to aim a camera on one tree from morning until night day after day, beginning with Spring when the tree begins to bloom, and to follow it through the cycle of Fall, Winter, Summer and renewed Spring, never letting the camera stop nor veer from its target—right on the tree, to catch each subtle change of growth and decline that the eye, moving restlessly from tree to tree or bush or person, cannot detect.

What then will we have? And what then will we be able to discover? But there is hope, plenty of hope that it will yield what we yearn to know. Oh how we long to know, as we live and as we die absolutely.

from *Boulevard*

Hourglass

◇ ◇ ◇

"Flawless" is the word, no doubt, for this third of May
that has landed on the grounds of Mayfair,
the Retirement Community par excellence.

Right behind the wheels of the mower, grass
explodes again, the bare trees most tenderly
push out their chartreuse tips.

Bottle bees are back. Feckless, reckless,
stingless, they probably have a function.
Above the cardinal, scarlet on the rim

of the birdbath, twinning himself,
they hover, cruise the flowers, mate.
The tiny water catches the sky.

On the circular inner road, the lady
untangles the poodle's leash from her cane.
He is wild to chase the splendid smells.

The small man with the small smile,
rapidly steering his Amigo,
bowls past. She would wave, but can't.

All around, birds and sexual flowers
are intent on color, flight, fragrance.
The gardener sweeps his sweaty face

with a khaki sleeve. His tulips are shined
black at their centers. They have come along nicely.
He is young and will be gone before dark.

The man in the Amigo has in mind a May
a mirror of this, but unobtainable
as the touch of the woman in that glass.

The sun's force chills him. But the lady
with the curly poodle could melt her cane
in the very heat of her precious pleasure.

She perfectly understands the calendar
and the sun's passage. But she grips the leash
and leans on the air that is hers and here.

from *The New Yorker*

Questions for Ecclesiastes

◊   ◊   ◊

What if on a foggy night in a beachtown, a night when
   the Pacific leans close like the face of a wet cliff,
   a preacher were called to the house of a suicide,
   a house of strangers, where a child had discharged
   a rifle through the roof of her mouth and the top
   of her skull?

What if he went to the house where the parents, stunned
   into plaster statues, sat behind their coffee table
   and what if he assured them that the sun would rise
   and go down, the wind blow south, then turn north,
   whirling constantly, rivers—even the concrete
   flume of the great Los Angeles—run into the sea,
   and fourteen-year-old girls would manage to spirit
   themselves out of life, nothing was new under the
   sun?

What if he said the eye is not satisfied with seeing,
   nor the ear filled with hearing? Would he want
   to view the bedroom vandalized by self-murder or
   hear the quiet before the tremendous shout of the gun
   or the people inside the house, shouting or screaming,
   crying and pounding to get into the room, kicking
   through the hollow core door and making a new
   sound and becoming a new silence—the silence he
   entered with his comfort?

What if as comfort he said to the survivors I praise
   the dead which are dead already more than the living,
   and better is he than both dead and living who is
   not yet alive? What if he folded his hands together
   and ate his own flesh in prayer? For he did pray
   with them. He asked them, the mother and father,
   if they wished to pray to do so in any way they
   felt comfortable, and the father knelt at the coffee
   table and the mother turned to squeeze her eyes into
   a corner of the couch, and they prayed by first
   listening to his prayer, then clawing at his measured
   cadences with tears (the man cried) and curses
   (the woman swore). What if, then, the preacher said
   be not rash with thy mouth and let not thine heart
   be hasty to utter anything before God: for God
   is in heaven?

What if the parents collected themselves, then, and
   asked him to follow them to their daughter's room,
   and stood at the shattered door, the darkness of
   the room beyond, and the father reached in to put
   his hand on the light switch and asked if the
   comforter, the preacher they were meeting for the
   first time in their lives, would like to see the
   aftermath, and instead of recoiling and apologizing,
   he said that the dead know not anything for the
   memory of them is forgotten? And while standing
   in the hallway, he noticed the shag carpet underfoot,
   like the fur of a cartoon animal, the sort that
   requires combing with a plastic rake, leading into
   the bedroom, where it would have to be taken up,
   skinned off the concrete slab of the floor, and still
   he said for their love and hatred and envy are now
   perished, neither have the dead any more portion
   forever in anything that is done under the sun?

What if as an act of mercy so acute it pierced the
preacher's skull and traveled the length of his
spine, the man did not make him regard the memory
of his daughter as it must have filled her room,
but guided the wise man, the comforter, to the front
door, with his wife with her arms crossed before her
in that gesture we use to show a stranger to the
door, acting out a rite of closure, compelled to
be social, as we try to extricate ourselves by
breaking off the extensions of our bodies, as
raccoons gnaw their legs from traps, turning aside
our gaze, letting only the numb tissue of valedictory
speech ease us apart, and the preacher said live
joyfully the days of the life of thy vanity,
for that is thy portion in this life?

They all seem worse than heartless, don't they, these
crass and irrelevant platitudes, albeit stoical
and final, oracular, stony, and comfortless?
But they were at the center of that night, even
if they were unspoken.

And what if one with only a casual connection to the
tragedy remembers a man, younger than I am today,
going out after dinner and returning, then sitting
in the living room, drinking a cup of tea, slowly
finding the strength to say he had visited these
grieving strangers and spent some time with them?

Still that night exists for people I do not know in
ways I do not know, though I have tried to imagine
them. I remember my father going out and my father
coming back. The fog, like the underskin of a broken
wave, made a low ceiling that the street lights
pierced and illuminated. And God who shall bring
every work into judgment, with every secret thing,

whether it be good or whether it be evil, who could have shared what He knew with people who needed urgently to hear it, God kept a secret.

from *New England Review*

Grand Projection

◇   ◇   ◇

Its huge numbers include us, our cars, houses, and substantial goods,
    but the numbers
Do not stop north of Lake George or south of the Rio Grande.
There is a large number that stands for the Atlantic.
There is a very large number that stands for the Pacific.
Last winter a number of Mexicans smuggling their muscles north
    in a shut railway car
Suffocated and was added to a larger number, which includes
    the teenage pregnancy and whooping crane,
And will it be enough, when the great condor and sea tortoise
    have shrunken to one,
To weigh the hour of ovulation against the bounty of the sperm?

It is not just the children to come. Also, the rat, the opossum,
    the raccoon, and the mourning dove
Have traveled the sewer main and, dead, mounted sufficient work
To be counted among the problems, which include the Mexicans,
    the Ethiopians, and acid rain.
Our problems are so numerous, it is very essential that we count
The boats, their size and type, and the numbers of life preservers,
    fire extinguishers, and horns.
And it must be clear, even to the forgotten and almost extinct Arapaho,
Why one of us must keep the books of the crows and the ledgers
    of the bees,
And, glumly, another counts the instruments after the failed operation
    as the final
Number is wired to the big toe, and the hands are crossed neatly.

Otherwise, the dark vector keeps on rising on that unlined graph,
        and we feel,
From far south, across the plunging of that gulf, in cities,
        uncharmable and vast,
Those streets where a number of the just deceased are left to rot—
There is no telling when the government trucks will come
        and pick up a token number,
No reckoning how many each of the deceased has disappointed,
How many children, crippled, clever, gifted, how many cooperative
        and uncooperative sexual partners.
The unnumbered fruits rot, unprofitable, shameful;
The coat of paint is left to peel, no command is given to recover it,
        and there is nothing to say
After the mortar attack, when the reporters go like maggots,
        working the torn nests.

Or if there is a story, say it was too much to say even a single
        palm tree, the shade of the mission
Where the old one-legged man cut tires into sandals,
Or those bluest of lakes cupped in the craters of dead volcanoes.
Say there were too many saints and holidays, too many small people
Following donkeys up roads that vanished into gullies and trees,
        too many siestas.
Say the mathematicians left, the multiplications were so various,
        and there was nothing left to divide.

But record these zeros, ripening on vines beyond the infected wells,
        look carefully
At the mountain devoid of trees, the men passed out on the streets,
And the women bending to irritate their stony rows of corn,
        for something
Like history is trying to take place in secret meetings and bombs,
Something that does not include us, though we are there in force,
        counting the dead,

And the aid we read of sending underwrites the new resorts
    we will visit perhaps,
When the sense of history is strongest, just after the peace is signed.

from *New England Review*

DONALD JUSTICE

Invitation to a Ghost

◇ ◇ ◇

for Henri Coulette (1927–1988)

I ask you to come back now as you were in youth,
Confident, eager, and the silver brushed from your temples.
Let it be as though a man could go backwards through death,
Erasing the years that did not much count,
Or that added up perhaps to no more than a single brilliant forenoon.

Sit with us. Let it be as it was in those days
When alcohol brought our tongues the first sweet foretaste of oblivion
And what should we speak of but verse? For who would speak of
      such things now but among friends?
(A bad line, an atrocious line, could make you wince: we have all
      seen it.)

I see you again turn toward the cold and battering sea.
Gull shadows darken the skylight; a wind keens among the chimney
      pots;
Your hand trembles a little.
                 What year was that?

Correct me if I remember it badly,
But was there not a dream, sweet but also terrible,
In which Eurydice, strangely, preceded *you*?
And you followed, knowing exactly what to expect, and of course she
      did turn.

Come back now and help me with these verses.
Whisper to me some beautiful secret that you remember from life.

from *Sewanee Theological Review*

The White Pilgrim: Old Christian Cemetery

◊   ◊   ◊

The cicadas were loud and what looked like a child's
Bracelet was coiled at the base of the Pilgrim.
It was a snake. Red and black.   The cemetery
Is haunted. Perhaps by the Pilgrim. Perhaps
By another.   We were looking for names
For the baby. My daughter liked Achsa and Luke
And John Jacob. She was dragging her rope
Through the grass. It was hot. The insect
Racket was loud and there was that snake.
It made me nervous. I almost picked it up
Because it was so pretty. Just like a bracelet.
And I thought, Oh the child will be a girl,
But it was not.   This was around the time
Of the dream.   Dreams come from somewhere.
There is this argument about nowhere,
But it is not true.   I dreamed that some boys
Knocked down all the stones in the cemetery,
And then it happened. It was six months later
In early December. Dead cold. Just before
Dawn. We live a long way off so I slept
Right through it. But I read about it the next
Day in the Johnsonburg paper.   There is
This argument about the dead, but that is not
Right either. The dead keep working. If
You listen you can hear them.   It was hot

When we walked in the cemetery. And my daughter
Told me the story of the White Pilgrim.
She likes the story. Yes, it is a good one.
A man left his home in Ohio and came East,
Dreaming he could be the dreamed-of Rider
in St. John's *Revelations*. He was called
The White Pilgrim because he dressed all
In white like a rodeo cowboy and rode a white
Horse. He preached that the end was coming soon.
And it was. He died a month later of the fever.
The ground here is unhealthy. And the insects
Grind on and on.   Now the Pilgrim is a legend.
I know your works, God said, and that is what
I am afraid of.   It was very hot that summer.
The birds were too quiet.   *God's eyes are like
A flame of fire*, St. John said, *and the armies
Of heaven* . . . But these I cannot imagine.
Many dreams come true. But mostly it isn't
The good ones.   That night in December
The boys were bored. They were pained to the teeth
With boredom. You can hardly blame them.
They had been out all night breaking trashcans
And mailboxes with their baseball bats. They
Hang from their pickups by the knees and
Pound the boxes as they drive by. The ground
Here is unhealthy, but that is not it.
Their satisfaction just ends too quickly.
They need something better to break. They
Need something holy. But there is not much left,
So that night they went to the cemetery.
It was cold, but they were drunk and perhaps
They did not feel it. The cemetery is close
To town, but no one heard them.   The boys are part
Of a larger destruction, but this is beyond
What they can imagine. War in heaven
And the damage is ours. The birds come to feed
On what is left. You can see them always
Around Old Christian. As if the bodies of the dead

Were lying out exposed. But of course they are
Not.   St. John the Evangelist dreamed of birds
And of the White Rider. That is the one
The Ohio preacher wanted to be. He dressed
All in white leather and rode a white horse.
His own life in the Midwest was not enough,
And who can blame him? My daughter thinks
That all cemeteries have a White Pilgrim.
She said that her teacher told her this. I said
This makes no sense but she would not listen.
There was a pack of dogs loose in my dream
Or it could have been dark angels. They were
Taking the names off the stones.   St. John said
An angel will be the one who invites the birds
To God's Last Supper, when he eats the flesh
Of all the kings and princes.   Perhaps God
Is a bird. Sometimes I think this. The thought
Is as good as another.   The boys shouldered
Over the big stones first, save for the Pilgrim.
And then worked their way down to the child-
Sized markers. These they punted like footballs.
The cemetery is close to town but no one
Heard them. They left the Pilgrim for last
Because he is a legend, although only local.
My daughter thinks that all cemeteries
Have a White Pilgrim, ghost and stone, and that
The stone is always placed dead in the center
Of the cemetery ground. In Old Christian
This is true. The Ohio Pilgrim was a rich man
And before he died he sunk his wealth into
The marble obelisk called by his name. We saw
The snake curled around it. Pretty as a bracelet.
But the child was not a girl.   The boys left
The Pilgrim till last, and then took it down,
Too.   The Preacher had a dream but it was not
Of a larger order so it led to little. Just
A stone broken like a tooth, and a ghost story
For children.   God says the damage will be

Restored. Among other things.   At least
They repaired Old Christian. The Historical
Society raised a collection and the town's
Big men came out to hoist the stones. The boys
Got probation, but they won't keep it.   I
Don't go to the cemetery anymore. But once
I drove past and my babysitter's family
Was out working. Her father and mother were
Cutting back the rose of Sharon, and my red-haired
Sitter, who is plain and good-hearted, was
Pushing a lawn mower. Her beautiful younger
Sister sat on the grass beside the Pilgrim
Pretending to clip some weeds. She never works.
She has asthma and everybody loves her.
I imagined that the stones must have fine seams
Where they had been broken. But otherwise
Everything looked the same. Maybe better . . .
The summer we walked in the cemetery it was hot.
We were looking for names for the baby
And my daughter told me the story of the White
Pilgrim. This was before the stones fell
And before the worked-for restoration.
I know your works, says God, and talks of
The armies of heaven. They are not very friendly.
Some dreams hold and I am afraid that this
May be one of them. The White Rider may come
With his secret name inscribed on his thigh,
King of Kings, Lord of Lords, and the child
Is large now . . . but who will be left standing?

from *The Gettysburg Review*

ROBERT KELLY

Mapping

◇ ◇ ◇

for Charlotte

A book for us to write, like this:
you'll uncap the pen and hold the barrel
you'll press the iridium nib against soft paper
you'll draw a line—extend
it to a word
it will run from your hip up your heart to your hand
and it will say.

And what do I do. I sit beside you and turn the pages.
Diminuendo then sudden fortissimo—
I know where I am in the world by loudness alone.

How will the book know when we write it
what it's supposed to say.
It says what it must say.
It is a single piece of paper, very large or infinite,
and everything has to be findable there,
metabolism of desert rodents,
ratio of fat to muscle in singing birds,
predators, swallowers of discarded flesh.

★

A man is bent double over the hood of a car
and the police are twisting his thick sunburned arms behind his back
putting handcuffs on.
Ambulances with swinging lights, sheriffs and troopers
and a street full of frightened people.

This has to be in the book. This is the map.
It has to show the fear, it has to show my hand
squeezing your wrist too hard, the doubt
beginning to show in your eyes as you look at me,
the grief in mine that I would twist the world again,
that I'm doing it again, hurt you to love me.
That I can't trust the world to come to me and stay.
Draw me this world I don't trust, draw me trusting it.

Hot thunder. Show me.
I am a man bent low
constrained by circumstance,
why is it so sad,
where does this grief come from
you hear in my voice,
what do I know that makes me grieving,
I grieve with an ancient remorse I don't understand,
draw me a map with me remembering, forgiving, with me letting
    go.
Thunder. Dark thunder. Dark hot thunder.
Light is full of conveyance.
Oh that was lightning, it touched you faintly.
Lit up the profile of my face like a flicker of remorse.

★

They all are, all are speaking,
petals   copper acetate   old names
of a sweet old chemistry
loving things with language
                    that now we only know by number

a celadon vessel tinged nudely with palest crimson
shaped like the square root of five.

★

Map our revelation.
When you decide where the mountains are
we can find the Grail Temple
thickening clouds over the grain elevator
a scrap heap and the gates
swing open out of solid gold

hands around your hips now squeezing too tight
what is between Chicago and the North Pole
you squirm in my hands
trying to get free trying to get closer to me
how will I ever know
I hold so tight
I crush all the old maps in my hands my strong
hands give me a new map draw me a mountain

how strong you make me
draw me a map of your root honesty lend it to me
measure it all the way back to the moon

this map now
we begin

I think with your hand

you feel your body press down,
Lex dead of AIDS and David's friend
and — dying of it,
the pressure talks up the prussian blue of your veins
until you draw the map
complete in all its rivers copses spinneys
                    man-built weirs

          copper mines   salt pans
          dotted lines for caves
                              bearing down and in
from staggering cliffs
you mark by a bundle of contour lines
     —always 57° down there
          inside the constant earth
                    midnight in San Francisco the cry of men

map the cry of them
desperate for your body all of your bodies

until you draw the map
                    with every bight cove fjord quarry
          all the Ragusas of dubious argosies
     jabbering lighthouses staining the dark

until you draw the map
          with every battle site pricked out with crossed swords
     the Christian ruins and the man of war
                    sunk in the harbor
               fouled anchors oil rigs spirit guides
     marking ley lines with eye chalk

until you draw the map complete
          with an old woman in Appleton
                    eating cheese on saltine crackers

this book of ours will not be finished, draw it,
it is the only book,
I am waiting for your map
to forgive me
to explain the silence of the world,

draw a mesa and a bed
a snake asleep on sandstone cold morning
draw hemlocks in Russia

---

draw the Vatican if there is one
a Pope legislating from the star Canopus
draw the men haunting the corridors of ancient buildings
draw the shadow the moon casts on the Plaza de Toros
    when all the drunks have come home
and the bull is bleeding to death outside the wooden wall

then draw the shadow the moon throws down on the earth
no one can see
but we feel it
hard on our shoulders
sometimes when we turn
to each other or look
the same way in the sky.

What way is that? How does the land know
what the map is making it do?
Which way does a word point
when we look through each other
whoever we are?
          And it goes there,
nobody's listening, let the word go,
let the map pour out of your hands
hurry,
      you know something you almost remember.

from *Grand Street*

JANE KENYON

Having It Out
With Melancholy

◊ ◊ ◊

*If many remedies are prescribed for an illness, you may
be certain that the illness has no cure.*
A. P. CHEKHOV, *The Cherry Orchard*

1. FROM THE NURSERY

When I was born, you waited
behind a pile of linen in the nursery,
and when we were alone, you lay down
on top of me, pressing
the bile of desolation into every pore.

And from that day on
everything under the sun and moon
made me sad—even the yellow
wooden beads that slid and spun
along a spindle on my crib.

You taught me to exist without gratitude.
You ruined my manners toward God:
"We're here simply to wait for death;
the pleasures of earth are overrated."

I only appeared to belong to my mother,
to live among blocks and cotton undershirts
with snaps; among red tin lunchboxes
and report cards in ugly brown slipcases.
I was already yours—the anti-urge,
the mutilator of souls.

2. BOTTLES

Elavil, Ludiomil, Doxepin,
Norpramin, Prozac, Lithium, Xanax,
Wellbutrin, Parnate, Nardil.
The coated ones smell sweet or have
no smell; the powdery ones smell
like the chemistry lab at school
that made me hold my breath.

3. SUGGESTION FROM A FRIEND

You wouldn't be so depressed
if you really believed in God.

4. OFTEN

Often I go to bed as soon after dinner
as seems adult
(I mean I try to wait for dark)
in order to push away
from the massive pain in sleep's
frail wicker coracle.

5. Once There Was Light

Once, in my early thirties, I saw
that I was a speck of light in the great
river of light that undulates through time.

I was floating with the whole
human family; we were all colors—those
who are living now, those who have died,
those who are not yet born. For a few

moments I floated, completely calm,
and I no longer hated having to exist.

Like a crow who smells hot blood
on asphalt, you came flying
to pull me out of the glowing stream.
"I'll hold you up. I never let my dear
ones sink!" After that, I wept for days.

6. In and Out

The dog searches until he finds me
upstairs, lies down with a clatter
of elbows, puts his head on my foot.

Sometimes the sound of his breathing
saves my life—in and out, in
and out; a pause, a long sigh. . . .

7. Pardon

A piece of burned meat
wears my clothes, speaks
in my voice, dispatches obligations
haltingly, or not at all.

It is tired of trying
to be stout-hearted, tired
beyond measure.

We move on to the monoamine
oxidase inhibitors. Day and night
I feel as if I had drunk six cups
of coffee, but the pain

stops abruptly. With the wonder
and bitterness of someone pardoned
for a crime she did not commit,
I come back to marriage and friends,
to pink fringed hollyhocks; come back
to my desk, my books, and my chair.

8. CREDO

Pharmaceutical wonders are at work
but I believe only in this moment
of well-being. Unholy ghost,
you are certain to come again.

Coarse, mean, you'll put your feet
on the coffee table, lean back,
and turn me into someone who can't
take the trouble to speak; someone
who can't sleep, or who does nothing
but sleep; can't read, or call
for an appointment for help.

There is nothing I can do
against your coming.
When I awake, I am still with thee.

9. WOOD THRUSH

High on Nardil and June light
I wake at four,
waiting greedily for the first
note of the wood thrush. Easeful air
presses through the screen
with the wild, complex song
of the bird, and I am overcome

with ordinary contentment.
What hurt me so terribly
all my life until this moment?
How I love the small, swiftly
beating heart of the bird
singing in the great maples;
its bright, unequivocal eye.

from *Poetry*

Looking at the Sea

◇ ◇ ◇

Stiff tone of death
in every wave
what more can wave have
save perhaps a little love
    MARSDEN HARTLEY

Not in anger does the sea
fold to the source of its gray waves
the tired boy; not in hatred
does it choke him.

Before and afterwards a weight
breaks each wave, but not remorse

nor does forgiveness move the tides
to coax the shriveled kelp and barnacles,
the stinking whelks to trust
the sea's embrace again.

We who travel with our feelings
can't believe the sea responds mechanically
to the earth's rotation or the moon
giving up another sliver every night.

White edging on the waves leads the eye
from horizon into shore, from rocks
to a plume of spray dissolving into blue
oblivion,

abandonment,
convincing evidence
that prior to this breath
we were protected;

just yesterday
seagulls sang like doves.

from *The Ohio Review*

Talking to Patrizia

◊ ◊ ◊

Patrizia doesn't want to
Talk about love she
Says she just
Wants to make
Love but she talks
About it almost endlessly to me.

It is horrible it
Is the worst thing in life
Says Patrizia
Nothing
Not death not sickness
Is as bad as love

I am always
In love I am always
Suffering from love
Says Patrizia. Now
I am used to it
But I am suffering all the same

Do you know what I did to her
Once?—speaking
Of her girlfriend—I kicked her out
I literally kicked her she was down on the floor and I
Gave her the *colpi di piedi* the
Kicks of my foot. She slided out.

She did this
To me promised to go on a trip
I am all waiting prepared
Suitcases and tickets
She comes and says her other friend finds out she
Can't go she guessed about it. I KICKED her out

Oh we are still together
Sometimes. But love is horrible. I thought
You might be the best
Person to talk to Patrizia since you
Love women and are a woman
Yourself. You may be right Patrizia

Said. But this woman who abandons
You I think you should
Disappear. Though maybe with this woman
Disappearing won't work.
I think not disappear.
It's too bad I don't know her

If I knew her if I could see her
Just for ten minutes—I'm afraid
If you saw her you might take
Her away from me. Patrizia
Laughs. No it hasn't happened to me
Thank God to like such young women yet

Why? When you are my
Age—still young—she
Is thirty . . . nine? you are close enough
To people very young to
Know how horrible they are
And you don't love them

You don't want to have anything
To do with them! Oh
Uh huh, I said putting

My hands down on the table and then off
Look at you excuse me but I have to laugh
At you sitting in this horrible

Restaurant at one o'clock
In the morning in a
City you don't want to be
In and why? For this woman
It is horrible I know but
Also funny

I know I said. Listen I have
An idea. Do you know her address? You know where
She lives? You should go there
Go and hide there
Outside her house
In the bushes

Then when she comes out
You jump out
You confront her. You will see
If there is love
In her eyes or not. It can't
Be hidden. You will know It can't be mistaken

This works This has always worked
For me. It won't work for me. I can't
Go and hide there It is true
Patrizia says when there is love everything
Works when there isn't, nothing does. Love
Is a god These Freudian things I don't believe at all

This god you have to do what
He wants you to you are
Angry but all you really want
Is to get her back. Then—revenge! If
This woman did something like this to me
I would simply dislike her in fact

I would hate her You may want to consider
Patrizia said that this woman is
Doing this to test you. No, I
Said. I know she's not. I know something. I feel
A hundred years old. Yet
You don't look so bad, Patrizia said.

Find another woman. I can't. I
Know Patrizia said. But one always thinks it
Is a good idea. But
If you can't you can't. I
Can't even eat
This food Patrizia I said.

I'm sorry I said Patrizia to be so
Boring I can't stop talking Forgive
Me. It doesn't bore me at all
Patrizia says It's my favorite subject
It isn't every day one sees somebody
In such a state you can help him by talking to stay
    alive

You know, Patrizia says if she
Does this thing to you now
She will do it again
And again so you'd better be ready
Maybe you can get the advantage
By saying she is right you

Don't love her Good bye You leave
However if you want her
You should go into the bushes
And surprise her when they see you
It always makes a difference
I can't go hide there Patrizia

That's insane. I went but not
Hiding and not confronting.
Patrizia: What did she say? I said
The same things. Patrizia said
Did you see love in her eyes? I said
No, I didn't. I saw

Something else. In Florence it's rainy
Her (relatively) short hair and
Her eyes along the Arno
The last time I'll ever see her again
As the one I am seeing again
When seeing again still has some meaning

It's finished Patrizia's saying
For now but don't worry
I think you will get her back
But it will be too late Oh Patrizia I
Let my back and head fall against
The chair Late isn't anything!

from *Poetry*

Harriet Feigenbaum
is a Sculptor

◊　◊　◊

She is building a model of a concentration camp complex. She has
not been to a camp but has seen an aerial model. What she noticed:
the symmetry, the exactness. As maids place pillows (these are
Harriet Feigenbaum's ideas, images), so was the concentration
camp complex: orderly, but not in relation to a plan. The comman-
dant's house with its kitchen was in the center—surrounded, then,
by the ovens, gas chambers. In high school, several of my teachers'
wives were in mental hospitals (asylums). No one said why, but it
was understood they had started menopause and gone mad. One
felt pity for these men, still devoted to their crazy, absent wives. I
am post-menopausal. My doctor, Chinese, finds it difficult to ex-
amine my heavy breasts for lumps. The ob-gyn I went to for an
abortion when I was pregnant, at forty, vigorously palpated my
breasts for milk, maybe (to give him the benefit of the doubt) to
see how far along I was. He hurt me. My Uncle Nat Lemler was
a prison guard. My Aunt Jeannie was the least attractive of all my
mother's sisters. Not that they were beauties, but she had absolutely
no beauty, almost as if she deserved the terrible man she was mar-
ried to, who would divorce her, the first divorce in the family. I
felt terrible seeing Aunt Jeannie, who lived in poverty, as the ugly
duckling of my mother's large family. The Vietnam War Memorial

was created by an artist who was not a veteran. Reconnecting with a man I loved forty years ago, the chance for a new start and new loss. Terrible dreams too disgusting to write.

from *Poetry New York*

Chariot

◇　◇　◇

for Varujan Boghosian

In this image of my friend's studio,
where curiosity runs the shop, and you
can almost smell the nostalgic dust
settling on the junk of lost mythologies,
the artist himself stays out of view.
Yet anyone could guess
this is the magician's place
from his collection of conical hats
and the sprawled puppets on a shelf,
the broken as well as the whole,
that have grown to resemble him,
or the other way round.
Butterflies, gameboards, and bells,
strewn jacks and alphabet blocks,
spindles, old music scores—
the litter spreads from wall to wall.
If you could dig to the bottom,
you might expect to find
a child's plush heart,
a shining agate eye.
Here everything waits to be renewed.
That horse-age wagon wheel
propped in the corner
against an empty picture-frame,
even in its state of disrepair,

minus three spokes,
looks poised for flight.
Tomorrow, maybe, at the crack of a whip
a flock of glittering birds will perch
on its rim, a burnished stranger
wearing an enigmatic mask
will mount its hub
and the great battered wheel
will start to spin.

from *The Gettysburg Review*

In California During the Gulf War

◇ ◇ ◇

Among the blight-killed eucalypts, among
trees and bushes rusted by Christmas frosts,
the yards and hillsides exhausted by five years of drought,

certain airy white blossoms punctually
reappeared, and dense clusters of pale pink, dark pink—
a delicate abundance. They seemed

like guests arriving joyfully on the accustomed
festival day, unaware of the year's events, not perceiving
the sackcloth others were wearing.

To some of us, the dejected landscape consorted well
with our shame and bitterness. Skies ever-blue,
daily sunshine, disgusted us like smile-buttons.

Yet the blossoms, clinging to thin branches
more lightly than birds alert for flight,
lifted the sunken heart

even against its will.
                            But not
as symbols of hope: they were flimsy
as our resistance to the crimes committed

—again, again—in our name; and yes, they return,
year after year, and yes, they briefly shone with serene joy
over against the dark glare

of evil days. They *are*, and their presence
is quietness ineffable—and the bombings *are*, were,
no doubt will be; that quiet, that huge cacophony

simultaneous. No promise was being accorded, the blossoms
were not doves, there was no rainbow. And when it was claimed
the war had ended, it had not ended.

from *American Poetry Review*

The Urinating Man

◇ ◇ ◇

Sometimes one of Erickson's patients phoned him in the middle of
the night.
One man, a college professor, had come to Erickson with a simple
question:
Why was the orgasmic response of the human male referred to as
"ejaculation"?
The man had a wife and two children, so Erickson asked him
What happened to *him* when he and his wife made love.
After a while, said the man, the semen flows out of your penis,
Just as if you were urinating.
Questioning revealed the man had wet the bed till he was twelve;
He had learned a penis was for peeing, and that's what he did.
But it was not Erickson's method to "probe" or deliver "insights."
He instructed the man on ways to enhance the feeling in his
penis.
He was to handle the various parts and identify their sensations;
He was to drill at exciting himself while restraining the pee-flow of
semen.
After a month the phone rang at midnight. "I did it," the man
said.
He had had an ejaculation, in bed with his wife, for the first
time.
He called again at one-thirty. "I did it again," he said.

I have never before repeated the story of the urinating man;
I have never paraphrased it, aloud or on paper.
The story of the urinating man is funny but frightening too—

To think of the pathetic egotism and embarrassment
Keeping him for most of his life from finding out why
The world spoke with confidence of geysers and the best he knew
    was a trickle.
Certainly he was "functional"—though his wife told Erickson
    later
Their sex life had suddenly improved the night he made the
    phone call—
The content of which, and its preceding therapy, forever kept
    secret from her.
Perhaps there is actually reason to fear, the things we fear are
    wrong with us
Are really wrong—
The assurances we assuage ourselves with
Are injunctions lest it be found out we *do* do things wrong,
We *are* secretly different from everyone else on earth.
The urinating man had told himself he was fine as he was.
He had fathered two children, so things were "working" at least;
His wife had never mentioned anything unusual.
The miracle is that the man *ever* asked his question,
Giving up a lifetime of carefully tested explanations
That must finally have begun to grow thin.

People are afraid of keeping secrets between their legs.
They are afraid to look there with a strong light
And then have nothing to compare with.
Some of them suspect that what is wrong with them
Is that they are sure something's wrong:
If they went to someone knowledgeable, like a doctor, a
    therapist,
And he or she said, absolutely nothing's wrong
And turned with that smirk doctors half-conceal
When a patient's worries have just been revealed as groundless,
How would they learn what the urinating man had to learn?—
How to make himself feel better without telling himself
    anything;
How to take himself into his hands.
It would be better to have someone make you do a thing like that.

Someone you knew could make you do it, like a doctor,
And would make you do it for a good reason,
Like a famous doctor; and money would change hands,
The idea being that the money would change hands.
If you had been one of Erickson's patients, say one of the last
    ones,
In the seventies, you would have contracted him for his services.
It might have meant his answering the phone at midnight
And again at one a.m.—and he was old, lamed all his life with
    polio.
You would pay to tell him intimate things,
The old, lame man; and then, because he was the doctor,
And paid to speak, he'd tell you something.

from *Poetry East*

Grim Town
in a Steep Valley

◊   ◊   ◊

This valley: as if a huge, dull, primordial axe
once slammed into the earth
and then withdrew—X millennia ago.
A few flat acres
ribbon either side of the river sliding sluggishly
past the clocktower, the convenience store.
If a river could look over its shoulder,
glad to be going, this one would.
In town center: a factory of clangor and stink,
of grinding and oil,
hard howls from drill bits
biting sheets of steel. All my brothers
live here, every cousin, many dozens
of sisters, my worn aunts
and numb uncles, the many many of me,
a hundred sad wives,
all of us countrymen and women
born next to each other behind the plow
in this valley, each of us
pressing to our chests a loaf of bread
and a jug of milk. . . . The river is low
this time of year and the bedstones' blackness
marks its lack
of depth. A shopping cart
lies on its side in center stream

gathering branches, detritus, silt,
forcing the already weak current to part for it,
dividing it, but even so diminished
it's glad to be going,
glad to be gone.

from *Field*

The Nearsighted

◊   ◊   ◊

who misreads the serious joke, the speech
as everyday speech, the smile as pleasure, the map
as a flat land, sooner for later,

who once could misread "the law," briefly,
as "lawn party," longing perhaps
to see the great at leisure—the great

leisurely great at leisure on a lawn
in its late-summer greens, in their
black robes. No matter. Quickly corrected:

"the law." Takes off her glasses in spring
to see the flowers—*vide* Impressionists—light, air
in the National Arboretum. It is a mass, a confection

of colors, of course: a stroll in perfection. Solemnly
curling new hybrid tulips are only gaiety, planted in thrilling
profusion, variety. Purely a vision. One hill section

of overgrown lawn, beyond a hedge, holds twenty-odd columns
standing transplanted, standing alone, that hold no building.
Once they stood (a sign) at the first Capitol. Benefactions

saved them (a list of donors), to bring them here. Here
freestanding, mis-seen at a distance, the scene could be
scenery for an ancienter demos, dead grandeur. Close,

their Corinthian capitals cast such intricate shadows
down their sides—was it acanthus?—even the nearsighted sees
the Founders' stoneworker's first

intention, a far-off gesture: Yes, we chose
to believe this way. But now, here. The nation's given us
acres. Not so far away, the narcissus

garden, its near-hidden signs among short leaves, calls
for corrective lenses. It sends its instructive paths
through a polleny wood, telling us, "This

is Our Temple, among the gold-centered
namesakes of Presidents and First Ladies. . . . That's
the frilled Ring Leader. . . . Burning Heart. . . ." Thus

the bedazzled flower breeders, lovers of Beauty
all—romantics—giving names to what they admired, what we had
        seen
as glorious, clean, benefaction. Not far off,

the tiny trees of the bonsai garden make each planting
a world. A nearsighted citizen finds six trees
in a foot-wide glade of beeches,

sees its minuscule guest, hears its minuscule
suppliants. Its invisible dryad. "This is pause
I give you, if I can—green hiatus

caught in a stone jar, just this far from magenta-
flowered truce in confusion, absurd azalea."
Foemina Juniper, white-dead branches spires

above a still-green forest—all just
inches tall—holds no natural fauna
the eye can see. The law

requires reason. Across a roadway, beds
of industrial herbs, medicinal herbs, et cetera,
smell as strong as sage. In the virtues of dittany

only the pungent, invisible gods believe. The
nearsighted sees bound water lilies in a popular pool
not far away, the civil golden carp

vague beneath them, and wants to believe there's no great
loss to be seen in this generation, no lost equilibrium, barely
a lost clear lost tradition.

from *The New Yorker*

Open Rebuke
(Concealed Love)

◊   ◊   ◊

1.

What we cannot solve
ourselves we share, a simple shift
of letter from irresistible
last light to first darkness.

Paranomasia contrarium.
I could not see my fingertips
in the darkness. The horse
I rode stopped as if in fear
of our being betrayed.

Trees revealed an alleyway
of sky whose light
was all that led us, leaning over
our embrace in

a friendly manner, brother and
sister, old enough
to interfere in other loves
whose sorrows
now were nothing

whose histories
had vanished. Then recoiled;
we were left
to complain of each other,

of the day we met.
Yet, reappearing, the trees bent
before us to ask
forgiveness for their lapse,
and our fate forgot

it was to fall. There is no
need to hide
from a story we understand. No
need to explain.

2.

The master's words are mutual,
exclusive miracles
of concealed love. Do not

cut the foundation
from under these words
that infatuate us,
but follow at a distance

of critical passion,
impregnable to their discomfort,
terse and tense.

Distance hides love and with
deflected affinity
rebukes excesses that sting
the cryptic name.

They have not seen the sun
          set miracles
a garment to adorn, nor lines

          on a hand lead
through a door to a creature
          whose hand it is,
preserving what we were told.

          Would I rejoin
what I left willingly moments ago?
          What we know

from a book, no need to ask
          of nature. An
Odyssey's no place to stage
          one's return.

3.

          To the refined and learned
aristocrats, gathered for wine,
          music and poetry,
the poet inside writing for himself
          only, or for his fellows,

has before him the model of their lives
          their real needs
ranging, in courtly lyric genre
          of love, praise,
wine and complaint, rhymed adages
          to delight the lords.

Idiosyncratic single realms
            selected to fuse,
sudden, emerge? Place breathes
            a hidden image of power,
sets the soul into its sighs.

            Exile, death.
Where does our land belong on
            this map? Go on,
are we one people, you
            with round hats
we bareheaded, leaning back?

            When the will turns,
as if one drew in breath,
            the soul returns
to its origin. One origin, exhalation,
            inhalation, then return.

Time began, and now at once
            it ends. Warriors
roar in the ramparts of words.
            A well-placed objection
explodes the wall. Wisdom ought not
            die, nor words

            live alone like hermits.
Enrich yourselves with others' breath.
            A story does not
dominate: to the crowd I give my
            heritage, to the mind.

4.

Grave, sufficient within itself,
            satisfied to be so,

consciously meditative and sober,
            purged of all
formal brilliance, eccentricity,

            of the surface
admired for itself, it renounces

            range of choice.
In a few meters its focus speaks
            resoundingly.

It neglects the inner disintegration
            (*anadiplosis, ut pictura*

poesis) of clear-cut ideas,
            perceptible, expected,
successive. Metaphor is its local

            ornament & conveys
its ideas in a new setting of words.

            However startling, every
image is fixed topos, feigning
            stimulation of the reader

in "*ostranenie*." The subject
            demands to be conveyed.

5.

We have no secret tradition
            to impregnate
the soul in creation. When we
            were lost, our

sciences too were lost. Set aside
         for a moment,
later what had been received

         could not be found.
A few memories remain, fragments
         shattered in the face
of philosophy's demonstrations.

         One example: Adam
sinned and fell from the wall;
         he broke into pieces.

To believe your own praise will
         kill you. All
"the king's men" could not put
         Adam together again.

No vessel contains a fluid
         more precious than
this lost body of secrets,

         an empty jar
we keep in our kitchen
         to recall
the good things it contained.

         from *Hambone*

1 5 2

From *The Person She Is*

◇   ◇   ◇

I know I'll lose her.
One of us will decide. Linda will say she can't
do this anymore or I'll say I can't. Confused
only about how long to stay, we'll meet and close it up.
She won't let me hold her. I won't care that my
eyes still work, that I can lift myself past staring.
Nothing from her will reach me after that.
I'll drive back to them, their low white T-shaped house
mine too if I can make them take her place.
I'll have to. I mustn't think her room and whether if by
nine one morning in a year she will have left it,
sleepy, late, remembering tomorrow is New York,
her interview with UN General Services a
cinch to go well. What I must think instead is Bobby's
follow-through from the left side. He pulls my lob past Geoff,
who's bored. Shagging five soaked balls isn't
Geoff's idea. I tell him he can hit soon. He takes his time,
then underhands the first off line and half way back.
Groundfog, right field, the freeway, LAX. She has
both official languages. For the International Court,
"The Registrar shall arrange to have interpreted
from French to English and from English into French
each statement, question and response." Or maybe it will be
Washington she'll work for. On mission to a new
West African republic, she might sign on with
Reynolds, Kaiser, Bethlehem Steel. They needed Guinea's
bauxite for aluminum, manganese from Gabon,

their dealings for more plants and harbors slowed by lengthy
phonecalls through Paris. When there were snags, she'd
fly there that same afternoon, her calendar a mix of
eighty hours on and whole weeks off. There'd be
sidetrips to England by Calais and one aisle
over from her on the crossing, by himself,
the man I saw this week I fear she'd like.
He'd have noticed her before they cleared the dock, she'd been
writing something, left wrist bent toward him, the card almost
filled, now, with whatever she'd been telling someone else.
She'd start another, the address first. Eased that he'd
sense it in his shoulders when she stood to leave,
he'd keep himself from looking, it was much better
not to look, he might not interest her, better
not to be left remembering how she looked.
Dover. He'd follow her to the train and sit
across from her, apply himself convincingly to his four
appointments and their dossiers. After she'd make
notes to herself from a bed and breakfast guide,
from *The Guide to the National Trust*, she'd put the books
back in her hemp bag. He didn't mean to be
nosy, he'd say, but was she going to
see some country houses while she's here? Comfortably,
she'd tell him which ones. Though he knew them all, he'd be so
taken with her that he'd lose what she was saying,
he'd undergo the list and ask if she'd be
hiring a car. She'd pick one up tomorrow in
Hammersmith and then drive west. Would she have
dinner with him tonight? She'd say she'd like that:
she was booked at the St. Margaret's, off Russell Square,
could he meet her there at seven? When she'd close her eyes,
her head against the cushioned wing of the seat,
he'd think her managing to rest was not so much a
carelessness to his attentions as that she wasn't vain.
She wouldn't catch him watching if he angled his look
away from her toward the window, in the tunnels
especially he'd see reflected in its glass her gradual
full outline as she breathed. There would be time all

evening to talk. He'd tell her then about his
uncle's place in Surrey where they'd both be welcome,
its rubble-stone and leaded casements, tile, an east
loggia to the lawns and wooded slope. He'd loved the
kitchen garden as a boy, the path there, silver
lavender and catmint borders, an oak-doored archway
framing for him on chains above a well the twin
coronas of roses in the cool damp light.

My wife is taking it well enough.
If there's another woman she doesn't want to know.
In LA, where no one knows us and would tell,
I rent a studio above a garage. Linda moves
out of the Y to the front unit of a duplex.
She's at the Ambassador for Bobby Kennedy's
victory party the night I leave. Dumbfoundedness,
one more impossible cortege, but she can come
over now, I can go see her, summer, our walks up the
fireroad in the last light, rabbits and even
deer sometimes across the reservoir on the grassy fans.
We go to the store together. There's time for
movies, now, and double solitaire. We wrestle.
She cuts my hair one Saturday outside her kitchen.

I have to teach again that fall and move back
down to Laguna. The days alone are less baleful,
they're just for a year. No one ever stops by,
but when she drives down on Thursdays after class
I meet her at the Tic-Toc Market. My apartment's
little more than the bed, and we can't wait.
Safe-harbored, whispering, with always more to tell,
we stay put, the dark catching up with us each week
until it's there in our first hour. From upstairs,
the muffled after-dinner clatter. Somebody's phone.
We start over at her knee, we're slower, the prolonged
fine sadnesses we'd hoarded from the years before
slow to give way and slowing so that only after
nothing for awhile does what we're doing take us

not toward her finishing again (or not right now) but
anywhere we've missed, her ribs, only the lightest
grazing of them, down and forward, not too far
nor too far back again across, each furrow
closer by its width to that last ridge below the pliant
dominating compass of her breast. We're being
pulled, of course. She hasn't stopped me. She won't.
At its outermost, her body's what she touches with.
It isn't long before she's moving too. Our skins
poised for the next just barely altered place, we're
thread-like stalks, light-running, sheer, our tiny leaves
flush with the basin's wide paved curb. It's still
gate-piered courtyard, ashlar dressed, a balustrade.
From jets above the circular pool alcoves,
water, its affection for an always lower point
tight-channeled in the iris rills, then underground,
the land dropping away through poplars to the dell.
Damp peaty banks easing to the full pond-hollow,
I'd never married, she'd been born to someone else.

from *TriQuarterly*

Waiting for Lesser Duckweed: On a Proposal of Issa's

◊   ◊   ◊

December, a weekday,
no one else crossing
    (by way of the wet path)

the bird santuary's yellow
spongy bottomland,
    no duckweed

any longer willow-green—
for now, the almost smoldering
    gas-lacy water says,

it's down making turions.
The way to be introduced to it
    is first

to meet nothing. In rain,
a thin microscope-specimen rain.
    One raises a face

to flooded sketchlike
territories of trees,
    sepia, seeping;

to blunt, upward bluffs of ivy,
bared poison oak;
        a soaking place,

fed by springs and floods,
shallow water table
        strained by willows.

In spring, in a more forward month,
yellow-red willow-bud husks
        will sharpen the trail,

their old pen tips,
oleo-spot gulls' beaks,
        brighten the flat brown pond,

and a man with a knife,
whack, whack,
        righthanded down the path,

will kill new twigs too new
yet to be woody.
        But there's

no duckweed until the summer
when finally where a creek
        swims in,

        there's duckweed
barely tugging
the moss-strandy bottom,

        wheatcolored
seed-shrimps
touring in and around

the barbless roots,
hyaline drag-lines,
where a mud-smooth leech adjusts

and tows
the duckweed a bit.
Some places it bunches,

simple but chained,
a soft hauberk on the stream.
Some places it wrinkles,

a basilisk's back.
It is utterly simple
and multiple.

It is floating,
one of many rafts.
The water here is cold,

fresh, still
and hard. Ovals, ovals.
"Let's take the duckweed way

to clouds,"
said Issa. Let's take it
when it comes to us,

its leaf
not called a leaf,
diameter for which there is no term

but green,
let's follow
the least weed up

to nimbuses
however many
steps it takes,

late in the day's
rootless endurance
to make much progress

the duckweed way.
Let us grow and wane
with this ideal, the way

it keeps the single petal
of its bloom confidential
in a hollow on its side.

Lemna minor

with thanks to Lucien Stryk,
who translated

from *The Iowa Review*

The Stranger

◇   ◇   ◇

After a Guarani legend recorded by Ernesto Morales

One day in the forest there was somebody
who had never been there before
it was somebody like the monkeys but taller
and without a tail and without so much hair
standing up and walking on only two feet
and as he went he heard a voice calling Save me

as the stranger looked he could see a snake
a very big snake with a circle of fire
that was dancing all around it
and the snake was trying to get out
but every way it turned the fire was there

so the stranger bent the trunk of a young tree
and climbed out over the fire until he
could hold a branch down to the snake
and the snake wrapped himself around the branch
and the stranger pulled the snake up out of the fire

and as soon as the snake saw that he was free
he twined himself around the stranger
and started to crush the life out of him
but the stranger shouted No No
I am the one who has just saved your life
and you pay me back by trying to kill me

but the snake said I am keeping the law
it is the law that whoever does good
receives evil in return
and he drew his coils tight around the stranger
but the stranger kept on saying No No
I do not believe that is the law

so the snake said I will show you
I will show you three times and you will see
and he kept his coils tight around the stranger's neck
and all around his arms and body
but he let go of the stranger's legs
Now walk he said to the stranger Keep going

so they started out that way and they came
to a river and the river said to them
I do good to everyone and look what they
do to me I save them from dying of thirst
and all they do is stir up the mud
and fill my water with dead things

the snake said One

the stranger said Let us go on and they did
and they came to a carandá-i palm
there were wounds running with sap on its trunk
and the palm tree was moaning I do good
to everyone and look what they do to me
I give them my fruit and my shade and they cut me
and drink from my body until I die

the snake said Two

the stranger said Let us go on and they did
and came to a place where they heard whimpering
and saw a dog with his paw in a basket
and the dog said I did a good thing

and this is what came of it
I found a jaguar who had been hurt
and I took care of him and he got better

and as soon as he had his strength again
he sprang at me wanting to eat me up
I managed to get away but he tore my paw
I hid in a cave until he was gone
and here in this basket I have
a calabash full of milk for my wound
but now I have pushed it too far down to reach

will you help me he said to the snake
and the snake liked milk better than anything
so he slid off the stranger and into the basket
and when he was inside the dog snapped it shut
and swung it against a tree with all his might
again and again until the snake was dead

and after the snake was dead in there
the dog said to the stranger Friend
I have saved your life
and the stranger took the dog home with him
and treated him the way the stranger would treat a dog

from *Poetry*

Rapture

◇　◇　◇

"Sing me something" is what the other keeps saying
night after night, regular as a pulse.

And when this one is alone, there's no problem.
He sings. He takes the lute-like
into his hands and plucks. Yes, he hears it.
What sounds like a sound. But when he opens his mouth,
it's different, it's the wrong sound.

Is it the acoustics inside
his head that make the difference? And who keeps
urging, making impossible demands
of him? "Come on,"

the other one is saying like
a faucet dripping, like a branch beating the window.
The window in his head. He opens it.

"Come on, Caedmon, sing me hwaethwugu." Yes,
that's how it sounds, like another
language, like gibberish, like
talking in his sleep. Remember the eensy-weensy

spider that climbed the water spout? That's how
he tries. His hands try. His lips.
It falls down. He tries. It falls down.
It's that regular. But when he makes it that regular
it's no good. It's not the same regularity.

I can't, he says, filling his mouth
with a big hole. Refusing, it begins for him.
Protesting, it swings itself up, it gets
going. It comes to him coming.

Or, it comes to her. What she lacks.
What hasn't happened in her
entire life, now it's coming, its absence
spread everywhere like a canyon in waves
of magenta and purple and gold.

The voice spreading before her. "Forget
outside. Forget sky outside and clouds outside."
This is what the voice spreads
before her, so she can look at what
it is saying. "Forget heaps of dirt and yellowish brown
dust and gravel." She passes through it,

a rift in her thinking where she lingers
so deeply and long
when she comes out of it, she can't remember
any more than a chasm spilling upward, clouds curling
an ocean of sound putting out stems
and branches of coral
which bend, break off, tempting

her body to match their motions. For a long time
she hears herself doing it, or I
hear her doing it,
in slow pendulations swept along, the bride
unbridling

in fetishistic foams and lace. The sound expanding
and stretching, blowing out
like bubble gum or Silly Putty.

The way a child flattens its nose and lips
against the glass of an aquarium
she pushes up against or I push up against
but when I go to say it, it sounds
different, hostile or angry with me, as if

I had seen
a gate opening in the dark
above my bed, a trellis on which light
grew and put out berries and thorns
of light and I

had blabbed instead of passing through.

from *Provincetown Arts*

April Fool's Day, Mount Pleasant Cemetery

◇   ◇   ◇

Snow lies in long bright fingers, frigid melt-water in pools.
The sun finds green in crushed grass newly uncovered and shining,
it warms the grey tombstones
while the city hums far away and high white buildings
stare down through bare trees. Alone, here,
it is possible to feel the proper sentiments,
love for the poor, contempt for the oppressor.
Then the young voices of two women approaching,
walking among the graves, talking and laughing softly:
rage floods back. The nearness of anyone,
the pleasant disturbing nearness of these girls,
their vowels like the poised mass of breasts
and motion of smooth hips . . . A moment ago
the ground here was covered with warblers
picking at last year's berries, coming near. They fled
and now they chatter far away. A crow lights in a maple,
the girls, never seen, are moving off behind the tangle
of yew, young spruce and cedar. And now again no one's here.
It seems that the birds, always searching in their disordered
anxious flocks, would come to be shepherded,
but these people never leave for long. Also the women
under the stones would come—this one "a victim

of the Lusitania," that one dead at thirty of God knows what:
if not for the voices that pass and never stop,
they would come out again and say what they were.

from *The Spoon River Quarterly*

Poppies

◊   ◊   ◊

The poppies send up their
orange flares; swaying
in the wind, their congregations
are a levitation

of bright dust, of thin
and lacy leaves.
There isn't a place
in this world that doesn't

sooner or later drown
in the indigos of darkness,
but now, for a while,
the roughage

shines like a miracle
as it floats above everything
with its yellow hair.
Of course nothing stops the cold,

black, curved blade
from hooking forward—
of course
loss is the great lesson.

But also I say this: that light
is an invitation
to happiness,
and that happiness,

when it's done right,
is a kind of holiness,
palpable and redemptive.
Inside the bright fields,

touched by their rough and spongy gold,
I am washed and washed
in the river
of earthly delight—

and what are you going to do—
what can you do
about it—
deep, blue night?

from *The Kenyon Review*

RON PADGETT

Advice to Young Writers

◇　◇　◇

One of the things I've repeated to writing
students is that they should write when they don't
feel like writing, just sit down and start,
and when it doesn't go very well, to press on then,
to get to that one thing you'd otherwise
never find. What I forgot to mention was
that this is just a writing technique, that
you could also be out mowing the lawn, where,
if you bring your mind to it, you'll also eventually
come to something unexpected ("The robin he
hunts and pecks"), or watching the FARM NEWS
on which a large man is referring to the "Greater
Massachusetts area." It's alright, students, not
to write. Do whatever you want. As long as you find
that unexpected something, or even if you don't.

from *The World*

Who Is To Say

◇　◇　◇

Who is to say
that the House of Tongues is not that place
where rats swarm around your feet
under blooming sofas

is not that place
of poisoned snows, pens run dry
and secrets now too late to know
and certainly the murmuring there below

was a mur-　was a mur-　was a
murmuring almost to be heard
a bubbling like water
invisible, underneath

And look the shadow of a wing
does fall here as blood
does drink deeply of itself
and does whisper yes for no

Once these faces behind glass
might have returned your glance
might even have gathered up
their limbs, in order to stand

Who is to say
that certain of their words did not spill out
as far as the eyes of cats could see
across the river in the dark

Leningrad
15 sept 90

from *Epoch*

LUCIA MARIA PERILLO

Skin

◇ ◇ ◇

Back then it seemed that wherever a girl took off her clothes
     the police would find her—
in the backs of cars or beside the dark night ponds, opening
     like a new leaf across
some boy's knees, the skin so white and taut beneath the moon
     it was almost too terrible,
too beautiful to look at, a tinderbox, though she did not know.
     But the men who came
beating the night rushes with their flashlights and thighs—
     they knew. About Helen,
about how a body could cause the fall of Troy and the death
     of a perfectly good king.
So they would read the boy his rights and shove him spread-legged
     against the car
while the girl hopped barefoot on the still-hot asphalt, cloaked
     in a wool rescue blanket.
Sometimes girls would flee so their fathers wouldn't hit them,
     their white legs flashing as they ran.
And the boys were handcuffed just until their wrists had welts
     and were let off half a block from home.

God for how many years did I believe there were truly laws
     against such things,
laws of adulthood: no yelling out of cars in traffic tunnels,
     no walking without shoes,
no singing any foolish songs in public places. Or else
     they could lock you up in jail

or, as good as condemning you to death, tell both your lower
    and upper case Catholic fathers.
And out of all these crimes, unveiling the body was of course
    the worst, as though something
about the skin's phosphorescence, its surface as velvet as
    a deer's new horn,
could drive not only men but civilization mad, could lead us
    to unspeakable cruelties.
There were elders who from experience understood these things
    much better than we.
And it's true, remembering I had that kind of skin does drive me
    half-crazy with loss.
Skin that to me now so much resembles a broad white lily
    on the first morning it unfurls.

from *Ontario Review*

Of Flesh and Spirit

◇ ◇ ◇

I was a virgin till I was 23. Then I always had more than one lover at the same time all secret.

In China, people are given the death sentence for watching a porno video while they can get free condoms and pills at any department store provided and mandated by law.

When my mother handed me my first bra which she made for me, I screamed and ran out the door in shame. She cut the bra into pieces because it was too small for her own use.

For 800 years, women's bound feet were the most beautiful and erotic objects for Chinese men. Tits and buns were nothing compared to a pair of three-inch "golden lotuses." They must be crazy or their noses must have had problems. My grandma's feet, wrapped day and night with layers of bandages, smelled like rotten fish.

The asshole in Chinese: the eye of the fart.

A 25-year-old single woman in China worries her parents. A 28-year-old single woman worries her friends and colleagues. A 30-year-old single woman worries her bosses. A 35-year-old single woman is pitied and treated as a sexual pervert.

The most powerful curse: fuck your mother, fuck your grandmother, fuck your great grandmother of eighteen generations.

One day, my father asked my mother if our young rooster was mature enough to jump, meaning to "mate." I cut in before my mother answered: "Yes, I saw him jump onto the roof of the chicken shed." I was ten years old.

Women call menstruation "the old ghost," the science book calls it "the moon period," and the refined people say "the moonlight is flooding the ditch."

My first lover vowed to marry me in America after he had my virginity. He had two kids, and an uneducated wife, and dared not ask for a divorce from the police. He took me to see his American Chinese cousin who was staying in the Beijing Hotel and tried to persuade his cousin to sponsor him to come to America. But his cousin sponsored me instead. That's how I am here and why he went back to his wife and is probably still cursing me.

Chinese peasants call their wives: that one in my house; Chinese intellectuals call their wives and concubines: the doll in a golden house; in the socialist system, husbands and wives call each other "my lover."

The story my grandma never tired of telling was about a man who was punished for his greed and had to walk around with a penis hanging on his forehead.

We don't say "fall in love," but "talk love."

When I left home, my father told me: never talk love before you are 25 years old. I didn't listen. Well, my first lover was a married coward. My first marriage lasted a week. My husband slept with me once, and I never saw him again.

from *The World*

Magic Problems

◊   ◊   ◊

The magician saws a woman in half,
pulls a rabbit from his shiny hat.
How did he do it? But we know
our pleasure requires not knowing how.
An amateur in the audience
would be looking for specific moves,
judging the trick on skill alone.
No fun for him, just homework.

When I was young I discovered
a way to prove that God exists.
Just let your mind go back
as far as possible, past the apes
and the volcanoes, past the fish with feet,
back to whatever first made thing
—a big stone, fire, air—you can imagine.
Then you call whoever made that "God."

No one was much impressed by this,
though it was comforting to think of God
inventing the world, not above me
watching what I did.
The magician finds a burning torch
in an empty paper bag—
a good trick, but frightening
if we didn't know about illusions.

Lightning blasts the dead tree—
we're confident it's not a sign.
When the stars assemble into human shapes
we remember their names,
or looking up at them now I know
where I left the book that would remind me.
A stick snaps not far away in the dark,
and because I've seen rabbits

at the edge of this small woods
I call it a rabbit. Then a creaking—
like a screen door being opened
where there is no door—which must be
the weight of a branch
on another branch.
Or a man, trying to stand
very quietly, adjusting his position.

from *Shenandoah*

ADRIENNE RICH

Not Somewhere Else, But Here

◇ ◇ ◇

WHAT KIND OF TIMES ARE THESE

There's a place between two stands of trees where the grass
                                          grows uphill
and the old revolutionary road breaks off into shadows
near a meeting-house abandoned by the persecuted
who disappeared into those shadows.

I've walked there picking mushrooms at the edge of dread,
                                          but don't be fooled,
this isn't a Russian poem, this is not somewhere else but here,
our country moving closer to its own truth and dread,
its own ways of making people disappear.

I won't tell you where the place is, the dark mesh of the woods
meeting the unmarked strip of light—
ghost-ridden crossroads, leafmold paradise:
I know already who wants to buy it, sell it, make it disappear.

And I won't tell you where it is, so why do I tell
you anything? Because you still listen, because in times like
                                          these
to have you listen at all, it's necessary
to talk about trees.

To the Days

From you I want more than I've ever asked,
all of it—the newscasts' terrible stories
of life in my time, the knowing it's worse than that,
much worse—the knowing what it means to be lied to.

Fog in the mornings, hunger for clarity,
coffee and bread with sour plum jam.
Numbness of soul in placid neighborhoods.
Lives ticking on as if.

A typewriter's torrent, suddenly still.
Blue soaking through fog, two dragonflies wheeling.
Acceptable levels of cruelty, steadily rising.
Whatever you bring in your hands, I need to see it.

Suddenly I understand the verb without tenses.
To smell another woman's hair, to taste her skin.
To know the bodies drifting underwater.
To be human, said Rosa—I can't teach you that.

A cat drinks from a bowl of marigolds—his moment.
Surely the love of life is neverending,
the failure of nerve, a charred fuse?
I want more from you than I ever knew to ask.

Wild pink lilies erupting, tasselled stalks of corn
in the Mexican gardens, corn and roses.
Shortening days, strawberry fields in ferment
with tossed-aside, bruised fruit.

AMENDS

Nights like this: on the cold apple-bough
a white star, then another
exploding out of the bark:
on the ground, moonlight picking at small stones

as it picks at greater stones, as it rises with the surf
laying its cheek for moments on the sand
as it licks the broken ledge, as it flows up the cliffs,
as it flicks across the tracks

as it unavailing pours into the gash
of the sand-and-gravel quarry
as it leans across the hangared fuselage
of the crop-dusting plane

as it soaks through cracks into the trailers
tremulous with sleep
as it dwells upon the eyelids of the sleepers
as if to make amends

MIRACLE ICE CREAM

MIRACLE'S truck comes down the little avenue,
Scott Joplin ragtime strewn behind it like pearls,
and yes, you can feel happy
with one piece of your heart.

Take what's still given: in a room's rich shadow
a woman's breasts swinging lightly as she bends.
Early now the pearl of dusk dissolves.
Late, you sit weighing the evening news,
fast-food miracles, ghostly revolutions,
the rest of your heart.

from *Southwest Review*

Makeshift

◊ ◊ ◊

I stood once at the tip of the earth,
Feeling myself no longer still,
But tossed with it about the sun
In an exquisite insecurity.

Behind me
Words
And the clothes of my sobriety
And people.

Before me
The sky
Parting like a curtain
Upon the ecstasy of all the universes beyond.

Oh, who was my unknown lover, there at the edge,
Come like a cloud to me,
Too large for my beholding?

I threw back my head for him
And he loved my throat
And brushed the tips of my breasts
And caressed my whole body,
Making me giddy with the sense of myself
And of the space about me
That was my lover.

Had I perceived too much?
Had my lover wearied of me so soon?
Or were my feet too quiet,
Planted perilously on the tip,
Too safe for leaping?

For the sky dropped again before me,
Formal and final as the end of a play,
And my words came to me again
And clothes
And people
And one among them, one of all others,
Who put his arms about me
And paid a ceremony to my lips
And to whom I answered:
I love you.

What else could I do,
Planted at the tip of the earth,
With my blossom lifted to the sky?
What else is left?

I will get me a child,
Another to yearn at the edge,
Better beloved than myself, perhaps,
Less secure, perhaps.

from *Chelsea*

Angels Grieving over the Dead Christ

◇   ◇   ◇

The epitaphios of Thessaloniki

From those few famous silkworms smuggled
Into Constantinople in the head of a walking stick
Silk waterfalls
Poured from the ancient bolts

Into now-destitute reservoirs
Of church treasuries in Aachen,
In Liège, in Maastricht, in Sens,
In the Sancta Sanctorum of the Vatican,

Bright rivers seeping past
The age when a teaspoonful of
Silkworm eggs the size of one grain
Could endow a church,

The age when the letters in the words
Of sacred testaments were
Unreeled in the coastal cities of Asia Minor,
When a bookworm conspired

To wrest a maze of empty roads
Through the words *My Lord*—
That ancient, flickering text
Once permanently affixed

By blind but face-picturing, speechless
But law-breaking wooden shuttles,
Now a heap of gold wires displayed
With a crumbling silk vestment someone

Plucked from a shovelful of dust
During one of those treasure hunts conducted
In the burying grounds, in other eras,
A shovelful of dust

Now blowing into your eyes,
As if a storm-wind from Paradise
Blew the rumors of His death
So hard you must cover your eyes

Before this museum case.
The late afternoon tugs
At a gold thread you can hear fraying
When you close your eyes,

A thread you feel your way along,
A thread at which the invisible globe pulls,
Leading you to the end of the world
Where there is a pile of

Clothes stolen from the grave,
Where your fear is relegated
To a masterwork of silk-gloves—
That He is dead.

Here death is only a flash of worlds
Unfurled from a rifled
Church-treasury, and you are invited
To walk this alluvial wave of gold,

To walk in the labyrinths
Of the angels' howls,
To run your hands along the walls
Of the silk thread's passageways,

To feel with your fingers
The angels' barbaric, stifled,
Glittering vowels
Tightly woven with gold wires.

If you were to tug at one,
Unraveling the angels
Into a vivid labyrinth of thread
From the fourteenth century

Backwards to the scissors-blade
A seraph takes to a fragile
Filament of gilt
According to a law still unrevealed,

The shroud would disappear
In the gust of a little breeze
From this door left ajar
Into the next life,

The threshold we cross with closed eyes—
Where angels hide behind their backs
The saws with which they mean
To saw the present from the past,

Oblivious to the scarlet threads
That prove to be hidden among
The filaments, those red rivers
Running through the theme of time

So shockingly—so before you set foot there,
Take heed. This is the work
Of Byzantine silk-slaves confined
To the palace grounds at Constantinople,

And you must beware.
There was a way station
On the Silk Road
Where the authorities executed

Traitors in a wooden box
In innumerable, unspeakable ways.
When you touch this shroud from the east
You take that hundred feet of road

You must walk softly past.
You must try not to look.
The torrent of words—later, later.
Here tongues are cut out,

And that is why the howling
Is mute,
Gilded, herringboned.
Because although this is death,

It is the work of slaves
Whose task was only
To expose the maximum amount of gold thread
To the ceiling price of so many nomismata

Per square inch, in a swift mischief
Of curious knots, of mazes
Flashing past, of straight paths
Made inextricable,

So look again.
The angels wring their hands
Over a statue. They are deranged,
But not by grief. They mourn

Not a body, but a work in bronze.
They do not bring a mortal to the grave.
But we onlookers who grieve and grieve—
We cannot relegate this thought

To a glory woven cryptically
In heavy silks,
We cannot consign it, sweep it off,
For we cannot weigh

In our palms the empty cocoons,
We cannot study
Within the secret workshops
Of the silkworm,

We cannot touch the boiling
Water where the spools whirl,
We cannot know firsthand
The bleakness of the craft

With which God made the world,
We cannot recount the legend that,
When they met face to face, both
God and the worm laughed.

from *The Yale Review*

Icon

◇   ◇   ◇

My father's photo in his dark-stained frame:
eight-pointed, etched star
at each notched vertex.
Boys High wood shop, circa 1920.

Teenage, old-master matrix
inferred from Poland's
martyrs above the candles
before he sailed here at six.

Object of meticulousness
for his meticulous, seamstress mother—
his wavy, impeccable hair; bowed lip;
light-flecked dark iris.

Almost myself as myself.
My gift from Aunt Florence the day
Uncle Nat's granite is unveiled.
Amen. Amen.

The Rabbi raised the cloth.
Stone not stone but love of unknowable God.
I nodded; I heard.
I wept but raged at a photo.

No son could do less.
Fists pressed to the eyes.
Puzzle of meticulous light closed to nothingness.
Forgive my father for he knows not.

Forgive my father for he knows not
that he tries
to halt Death in the wood shop.
He worked; took night school;

helped his hard, jobless father.
And his mother love told untold times.
Thus, he was my hard mother
when Mother was depressed.

Amen. Amen.
Nowhere to sit under the Zion noon
before Nat's grave dandelions.
Small stones put on the footstone,

for why one weeps or not.
And we drove Florence back through eternal Brooklyn.
A child consecrated us
on Cooper with a hydrant.

And I touched the waters
forgiving of the guilt unforgiven by what self
for anger at the father?
Father. Dearest friend.

Amen. Amen.
Perhaps this is God's axiom:
each day does not stop the errors
between this one and this one.

And there is no rebuttal.
Only birth, story.
Only barter: one thing for the next.
Only the four starred crosses of the matrix.

from *Pequod*

CHARLES SIMIC

This Morning

◇ ◇ ◇

Enter without knocking, hard-working ant.
I'm just sitting here mulling over
What to do this dark, overcast day?
It was a night of the radio turned down low,
Fitful sleep, vague, troubling dreams.
I woke up lovesick and confused.
I thought I heard Estella in the garden singing
And some bird answering her,
But it was the rain. Dark tree tops swaying
And whispering. "Come to me my desire,"
I said. And she came to me by and by,
Her breath smelling of mint, her tongue
Wetting my cheek, and then she vanished.
Slowly day came, a gray streak of daylight
To bathe my hands and face in.
Hours passed, and then you crawled
Under the door, and stopped before me.
You visit the same tailors the mourners do,
Mr. Ant. I like the silence between us,
The quiet—that holy state even the rain
Knows about. Listen to her begin to fall,
As if with eyes closed,
Muting each drop in her wild-beating heart.

from *The New Yorker*

Suddenly

◇   ◇   ◇

Nipkow and Cosulich
exported "seconds," merchandise
with small imperfections . . .
nylon stockings, ballpoint pens.
I packed them in cellophane,
then cartons, to be shipped
to Europe for their postwar legs
and literary movements.

Nipkow had a sideline, diamonds.
He would sit at his desk by the hour
holding a diamond up to the light
or staring at some little diamonds
in the palm of his left hand.
He'd rise and grind a diamond
on the wheel. Then put on his coat
and go to meet someone like himself
with whom he would exchange diamonds,
each of them making a profit
somehow out of this.

One day I suddenly quit.
Then I worked on the *Herald Tribune*.
A reporter would call "Copyboy!"
and one of us would run over
and take his copy to the horseshoe
where the Count, as we named him,

a bald head and rimless glasses,
presided over his crew.
One would read the piece in a hurry
and write a heading for it,
so many letters, to fit.

My greatest adventure
was going to the fourteenth floor
of the Waldorf-Astoria
to fetch copy about the flower show
at Madison Square Garden.

I quit that job suddenly too.
"You didn't like the export business,"
said Sylvia Cosulich—
I was still seeing her
though her parents didn't approve—
"and you don't want to be a reporter.
What are you going to do?"

In the silence there were sounds
of the traffic down below,
the elevator opening.

              Suddenly
the room seemed far away.
I was looking through a window
at clouds and trees.

And looking down again
to write, as I am now.

from *The Hudson Review*

Ripples on the Surface

◊　◊　◊

"Ripples on the surface of the water
were silver salmon passing under—different
from the sorts of ripples caused by breezes"

A scudding plume on the wave—
a humpback whale is
breaking out in air up
gulping herring
　　　—Nature not a book, but a *performance*, a
high old culture

Ever-fresh events
scraped out, rubbed out, and used, used, again—
the braided channels of the rivers
hidden under fields of grass—

The vast wild.
　　the house, alone.
the little house in the wild,
　　the wild in the house.

both forgotten.

No nature.

Both together, one big empty house.

from *Grand Street*

Coleman Valley Road

◇ ◇ ◇

This is where I had my sheep vision,
in the brown grass, under the stars.
I sat there shivering, fumbling with my paper,
losing tobacco. I was a spark at the most,
hanging on to my glasses, trying to hide
from the wind. This is how I bent

my head between my knees, the channels and veins
pumping wildly, one leg freezing, one leg
on fire. That is the saxophone
and those are the cymbals; when it gets up here
the roar of the waves is only a humming, a movement
back and forth, some sloshing we get used to.

That is my cello music and those are my headlights
making tunnels in the grass; those are
the clouds going down and those are the cliffs going out.
I am reaching up. I think I have
a carp's face, I have a round nose
and a large red eye and a ragged white mustache.

The strings are stretched across the sky; one note
is almost endless—pitiless I'd say—
except for the slight sagging; one note is

like a voice, it almost has words, it sings
and sighs, it cracks with desire, it sobs with fatigue.
It is the loudest sound of all. A shrieking.

from *Black Warrior Review*

That Winter

◇   ◇   ◇

In Chicago near the lake, on the North Shore,
your shotgun apartment has a sun room
where you indulge in a cheap
chaise lounge—
and read *Of Human Bondage*—
There is a window in the living room proper,
cracked open so your
Persian cat can go outside.
You are on the first floor and upstairs
a loud-mouthed southern woman
whose husband is away
all week on business trips
has brought her maid
up from Georgia
to do the work and take care of the baby.
"O lord," the southern woman says,
"He wants it spotless on the weekend—"
The maid, who has
smooth brown skin,
is not allowed to sit on the toilet
but she feeds the kid
and changes the dirty diapers.
She washes the dishes,
she cooks the southern meals,
she irons the sheets for the mahogany bed.
The southern woman shouts
at her in a southern drawl,

"Junie, don't sit on that chair
you'll bust it."
The southern woman is at
loose ends five days
waiting for him to come in.
"It's like a honeymoon,
honey," she says—
"When he grabs me,
whooee."
She invites you up and makes
sure you understand
the fine points of being a white woman.
"I can't let her live
here—not in Chicago.
I made her go out
and get herself a room.
She's seventeen.
She bellered and blubbered.
Now I don't know
what she's trackin' in
from men."
It is winter. The ice
stacks up around the
retaining wall—
the lake slaps over
the park benches,
blocks of ice green with algae.
You are getting your mail secretly at a postal box
because your lover is in the Aleutians.
It's during the war and
your disgusting husband
works at an oil refinery
on the South Side.
Up there in the Aleutians
they are knocking the gold
teeth out of the dead Japanese.
One construction worker
has a skin bag with fifty

gold-filled teeth.
He pours them out at
night in his Quonset hut.
He brags about bashing their faces in.
One day you are fooling
around in a downtown music store
waiting for the war to end.
You let a strange teenage boy
talk you into going
home with him.
He lives alone in a basement behind a
square of buildings.
He shows you his knife collection
and talks obsessively about Raskolnikov—suddenly
your genes want to live
and you pull away
and get out of there.
It is almost dusk.
You run until you find the boulevard
sluggish with the 1943 traffic.
You know by now there
isn't much to live for
except to spite Hitler—
the war is so lurid
that everything else is dull.

From *American Poetry Review*

From *Dark Harbor*

◇ ◇ ◇

I

Out here, dwarfed by mountains and a sky of fires
And round rocks, in the academy of revelations
Which gets smaller every year, we have come

To see ourselves as less and do not like
Shows of abundance, descriptions we cannot believe,
When a simple still life—roses in an azure bowl—does fine.

The idea of our being large is inconceivable,
Even after lunch with Harry at Lutèce, even after
Finishing *The Death of Virgil*. The image of a god,

A platonic person, who does not breathe or bleed,
But brings whole rooms, whole continents to light,
Like the sun, is not for us. We have a growing appetite.

For littleness, a piece of ourselves, a bit of the world,
An understanding that remains unfinished, unentire,
Largely imperfect so long as it lasts.

II

Is it you standing among the olive trees
Beyond the courtyard? You in the sunlight
Waving me closer with one hand while the other

Shields your eyes from the brightness that turns
All that is not you dead white? Is it you
Around whom the leaves scatter like foam?

You in the murmuring night that is scented
With mint and lit by the distant wilderness
Of stars? Is it you? Is it really you

Rising from the script of waves, the length
Of your body casting a sudden shadow over my hand
So that I feel how cold it is as it moves

Over the page? You leaning down and putting
Your mouth against mine so I should know
That a kiss is only the beginning

Of what until now we could only imagine?
Is it you or the long compassionate wind
That whispers in my ear: alas, alas?

III

I recall that I stood before the breaking waves,
Afraid not of the water so much as the noise,
That I covered my ears and ran to my mother

And waited to be taken away to the house in town
Where it was quiet, with no sound of the sea anywhere
    near.
Yet the sea itself, the sight of it, the way it spread

As far as we could see, was thrilling.
Only its roar was frightening. And now years later
It is the sound as well as its size that I love

And miss in my inland exile among the mountains
That do not change except for the light
That colors them or the snows that make them remote

Or the clouds that lift them, so they appear much higher
Than they are. They are acted upon and have none
Of the mystery of the sea that generates its own changes.

Encounters with each are bound to differ,
Yet if I had to choose I would look at the sea
And lose myself in its sounds which so frightened me
    once,

But in those days what did I know of the pleasures of loss,
Of the edge of the abyss coming close with its hisses
And storms, a great watery animal breaking itself on the
    rocks,

Sending up stars of salt, loud clouds of spume.

From *The New Republic*

In My Own Backyard

◇   ◇   ◇

I've seen fox, deer, wild turkey, pheasant, skunk,
snakes, moles, guinea hens. I've thrown a boomerang
that never came back.

I've played croquet, badminton, wiffle ball, frisbee.
My flower garden has never amounted to much, but there it is,
black-eyed Susans and tiger lilies pushing up
against the odds.

There's an old weathered chicken-coop full
of empty paint cans, a homemade wooden wheelbarrow.

Beyond that is an ersatz compost heap—I'm not consciously
composting anything.

A mulberry tree, a red maple, a spirea bush.

My neighbor hits a golf ball into my yard once in a while.
I watch him from the kitchen window.
I share a laundry line with him and his wife.
We catch up on neighborhood news about once a year:
he died, she left him, they took a trip to Canada.

Sometimes I walk the property line, first the side
adjacent to the forest, past the birch trees
and disused doghouse, then along the vacant field
where local kids played softball forty years ago—
the pitcher's rubber is still in place.

I try to appear as if I am inspecting something in the grass,
but I am a little daft, touched, as they say,
a little on my way out to pasture.

I grab my throat and wrestle me to the ground.
"There, there," I say, "lighten up ol' boy."
"It's a free country, it's your own backyard."
I listen intently: sky and daisies burlesque each other,

bivouacked between worlds.

from *American Poetry Review*

To a Former Mistress,
Now Dead

◊　◊　◊

Dear X, you wouldn't believe how curious
my eyebrows have become—jagged gray wands
have intermixed with the reddish-brown, and poke
up toward the sun and down into my eye.
It hurts, a self-caress that brings tears
and blurred vision. Aches and pains! The other day
my neck was so stiff I couldn't turn my head
to parallel-park; another man
would have trusted his mirrors, but not I;
I had the illusion something might interpose
between reality and its reflection, as happened with us.

The aging smell, X—a rank small breeze wafts upward
when I shed my underwear. My potency,
which you would smilingly complain about,
has become as furtive as an early mammal.
My hair shows white in photographs, although
the barber's clippings still hold some brown.
At times I catch myself making that loose mouth
old people make, as if one's teeth don't fit,

without being false. *You're well out of it—*
I tell you this mentally, while shaving
or putting myself to bed, but it's a lie.

from *Poetry*

Song and Story

◇   ◇   ◇

for Allen Grossman

The girl strapped in the bare mechanical crib
does not open her eyes, does not cry out.
The glottal tube is taped into her face;
bereft of sound, she seems so far away.
But a box on the stucco wall, wired to her chest,
televises the flutter of her heart—
news from the pit—her pulse rapid and shallow,
a rising line, except when her mother sings,
outside the bars: whenever her mother sings
the line steadies into a row of waves,
song of the sea, song of the scythe

      old woman by the well, picking up stones
      old woman by the well, picking up stones

When Orpheus, beating rhythm with a spear
against the deck of the armed ship, sang
to steady the oars, he borrowed an old measure:
broadax striking oak, oak singing back,
the churn, the pump, the shuttle sweeping the warp
like the waves against the shore they were pulling toward.
The men at the oars saw only the next man's back.
They were living a story—the story of desire,
the rising line of ships at war or trade.
If the sky's dark fabric was pierced by stars,

they didn't see them; if dolphins leapt from the water,
they didn't see them. Sweat beaded their backs
like heavy dew. But whether they came to triumph
or defeat, music ferried them out
and brought them back, taking the dead and wounded
back to the wave-licked, smooth initial shore,
song of the locus, song of the broom

> old woman in the field, binding wheat
> old woman by the fire, grinding corn

When Orpheus, braiding rushes by the stream,
devised a song for the overlords of hell
to break the hearts they didn't know they had,
he drew one from the olive grove—
the raven's hinged wings from tree to tree,
whole flocks of geese crossing the ruffled sky,
the sun's repeated arc, moon in its wake:
this wasn't the music of pain. Pain has no music,
pain is a story: it starts,
Eurydice was taken from the fields.
She did not sing—you cannot sing in hell—
but in that viscous dark she heard the song
flung like a rope into the crater of hell,
song of the sickle, song of the hive

> old woman by the cradle, stringing beads
> old woman by the cradle, stringing beads

The one who can sing sings to the one who can't,
who waits in the pit, like Procne among the slaves,
as the gods decide how all such stories end,
the story woven into the marriage gown,
or scratched with a stick in the dust around the well,
or written in blood in the box on the stucco wall—
look at the wall:
the song, rising and falling, sings in the heartbeat,
sings in the seasons, sings in the daily round—

even at night, deep in the murmuring wood—
listen—one bird, full-throated, calls to another,
little sister, frantic little sparrow under the eaves.

From *The Atlantic Monthly*

SUSAN WHEELER

A Filial Republic

◇ ◇ ◇

And out on the plaza, there were more people
Than had been expected: the aviators, with their
Thick dark muffs; the women in red, clapping
For Coca-Cola; the small trumpet player,
Leaning on the fender of the car which was not his;
The mechanics, spreading flat the manuals
For timing and for gaps; the blue majorettes;
The mother, who wished so hard she broke in two;
Those divided against the rule; Mick Jagger;
The security-green police; the gentle inquisitor;
The woman who had not yet found the voice for tragedy;
The exercise cadet, with Adidas and cassettes;
The deaf man, elegant, who bends to tie
His shoe; the grocery clerks, hanging back,
Aloof; the girls who clutched their T-shirts
From behind; the model with the cordless telephone;
The guests of honor, in their limousine;
The New Yorker hack; the derelicts, smitten with their
Own advice; the shampooer; the plasterer; the
Dishwasher; the drunk; the man so sodden with sex
He reeled; the crook; the benevolent sister;
The priest, wistfully; Allen Funt;
The father, crying with desire; the great
Conquistadors; the dreamers, who looked past the crowd
As it rolled in the sun; and the children:
Exclaiming together, as one hut and then another,
South, on the horizon, burst into fire.

Rise up, from where you are seated, smoking,
At a wooden desk. There has been a terrible dream
In the apartment above you, and the tenant is pacing.

from *No Roses Review*

C. K. WILLIAMS

A Dream of Mind: The Gap

◇   ◇   ◇

So often and with such cruel fascination I have dreamed the
      implacable void that contains dream.
The space there, the silence, the scrawl of trajectories tracked,
      traced, and let go;
the speck of matter in nonmatter; sphere, swing, the puff of
      agglutinate loose-woven tissue;
the endless pull of absence on self, the sad molecule of the self in its
      chunk of duration;
the desolate grain, flake, fragment of mind that thinks when the
      mind thinks it's thinking.
So often, too, with equal absorption, I have dreamed the end of it
      all: mind, matter, void.
I'm appalled, but I do it again, I dream it again, it comes uncalled
      for but it comes, always,
rising perhaps out of the fearful demands consciousness makes for
      linkage, coherence, congruence,
connection to something beyond, even if dread: mystery
      exponentially functioned to dread.
Again, premonitions of silence, the swoop through a gulf that
      might be inherent in mind
as though mind bore in its matter its own end and the annulment of
      everything else.
Somehow I always return in the dream from the end, from the
      meaningless, the mesh of despair,
but what if I don't once, what if the corrections fail once and I can't
      recover the thread

that leads back from that night beyond night that absorbs night as
    night absorbs innocent day?
The whole of being untempered by self, the great selves beyond self
    all wholly wound out;
sense neutered, knowledge betrayed: what if this is the real end of
    dream, facing the darkness
and subjecting the self yet again to imperious laws of doubt and
    denial which are never repealed?
How much can I do this, how often rejuvenate and redeem with
    such partial, imperfect belief?
So often, by something like faith, I'm brought back in the dream;
    but this, too; so often this, too.

from *The Threepenny Review*

The Business of Love is Cruelty

◇   ◇   ◇

It scares me the genius we have
for hurting one another. I'm seven,
as tall as my mother kneeling and
she's kneeling and somehow I know

exactly how to do it, calmly,
enunciating like a good actor projecting
to the last row, shocking the ones
who've come in late, cowering

out of their coats, sleet still sparkling
on their collars, the voice nearly licking
their ears above the swordplay and laments:
I hate you.

Now her hands are rising to her face.
Now the fear done flashing through me,
I wish I could undo it, take it back,
but it's a question of perfection,

carrying it through, climbing the steps
to my room, chosen banishment, where
I'll paint the hair of my model
Bride of Frankenstein purple and pink,

heap of rancor, vivacious hair
that will not die. She's rejected
of course her intended, cathected
the desires of six or seven bodies

onto the wimp Doctor. And Herr Doktor,
what does he want among the burning villages
of his proven theories? Well, he wants
to be a student again, free, drunk,

making the cricket jump, but
his distraught monster's on the rampage
again, lead-footed, weary, a corrosive
and incommunicable need sputtering

his chest, throwing oil like a fouled-up
motor: how many times do you have to die
before you're really dead?

from *Poetry East*

CONTRIBUTORS'
NOTES AND
COMMENTS

A. R. AMMONS was born in Whiteville, North Carolina, in 1926. He teaches at Cornell University and resides in Ithaca, New York. His most recent books are *Garbage* (1993) and *The Really Short Poems of A. R. Ammons* (1991), both from Norton. He received the Lannan Poetry Award in 1992.

Ammons writes: "I wrote 'Garbage' in the late spring of 1989. Because of some medical problems that developed soon after the poem was written, I didn't send it anywhere for a long time. The *American Poetry Review* very generously accepted it but because of a backlog had to delay publication for a while. By Capote's view, the poem is typing, not writing. I wrote it for my own distraction, improvisationally: I used a wide roll of adding machine tape and tore off the sections in lengths of a foot or more. The whole poem is over eighty pages long, so I sent only the first five sections to *APR*. Norton will publish the whole poem as a book in 1993. I've gone over and over my shorter poems to try to get them right, but alternating with work on short poems, I have since the sixties also tried to get some kind of rightness into improvisations. The arrogance implied by getting something right the first time is incredible, but no matter how much an ice skater practices, when she hits the ice it's all a one-time event: there are falls, of course, but when it's right, it seems to have been right itself."

JOHN ASHBERY was born in Rochester, New York, in 1927. He is the author of fourteen books of poetry, including *Hotel Lautréamont* (Knopf, 1992) and *Flow Chart* (Knopf, 1991). His *Self-Portrait in a Convex Mirror* (Viking, 1975) received the Pulitzer Prize for poetry as well as the National Book Critics Circle Award and the National

Book Award. A volume of art criticism, *Reported Sightings*, appeared in 1989 (Knopf). That was the year he delivered the Charles Eliot Norton lectures at Harvard University. He is currently Charles P. Stevenson, Jr. Professor of Languages and Literature at Bard College. He was the guest editor of *The Best American Poetry 1988.*

MICHAEL ATKINSON was born in Sayville, Long Island, in 1962. He currently lives in Lynbrook, New York, and works as a film critic in Manhattan writing for *New York Press, Movieline, Film Comment,* and *City Paper* (Baltimore). He won a 1988–89 fellowship from the New York Foundation for the Arts, and has had poems in *Crazyhorse, Prairie Schooner, Ontario Review, New Letters, Chicago Review, The Seneca Review, Hiram Poetry Review,* and numerous other publications.

Of "The Same Troubles with Beauty You've Always Had," Atkinson writes: "The poem is self-evidently a true story, excavating/carbon-dating an old friendship like the fossilized fly-in-amber such friendships inevitably become. I'm not the sort of poet who instinctively translates a visit to an abortion clinic into a poem; I didn't give it a thought until years later, after the relationship with my friend had settled into the long-distance affair the first part of the poem describes. Though unquestionably sympathetic, the poem's not terribly flattering, and I still have not given it to her to read—unfortunately, my habit seems to be write first, ask questions later.

"This is one of more than a hundred poems I wrote on company time during a cortex-numbing copy-editing day job; I worked on poems with my left hand while I edited law books with my right, and thus preserved myself for better days. As for formal considerations, there aren't many, and that's the way I like it—as far as I'm concerned, anyone can use a thesaurus or count beats (and count them *well*). I prefer to keep the craft invisible, in Philip Levine's words, and rely on the human meat of a poem—of the language—to pass the word."

STEPHEN BERG was born in Philadelphia in 1934. He founded *American Poetry Review* twenty years ago and is one of the magazine's three coeditors. His most recent books are *In It* (University of Illinois, 1983), *Crow With No Mouth: Ikkyu* (Copper Canyon Press, 1989), and *Behind Us: New and Selected Poems* (Copper Canyon, 1991). *Shaving* (prose poems) and *A Saint of the Ordinary* (prose diary) are in progress. In spring 1993 Philadelphia's Wilma Theatre presented his cotranslation (with Diskin Clay) of Sophocles' *Oedipus the King* in the vacant First Pennsylvania Bank at Fifteenth and Chestnut. Berg teaches at the University of the Arts.

Berg writes: " 'Cold Cash' was written as a birthday present for a friend. Perhaps it was an attempt to cheer her up. It revels in and mocks the power of money, the 'Oh, it's just beautiful!' rooms in *House & Garden*. It also uses the glamour of expensive objects as a setting for more serious concerns: death, love, etc. Somehow the surreal style in response to a long session on the toilet reading *HG* triggered the discourse. The birthday girl happens to love beautiful things. So do I. Doesn't everyone? The sonorities of impossible love. Dreams of salvation. The nightmare of unacceptable paradox. The escape from tragic emotion through shopping. The unbelievable degree of poverty and suffering everywhere. Photographs of Tolstoi dressed as a peasant make me sick. I prefer Chekhov in bed nursing his TB. I prefer the helpless euphoria of 'Cold Cash' to some of my failed poetic exercises in 'depth.' "

SOPHIE CABOT BLACK was born in New York City in 1958 and was raised on a small farm in New England. She attended Marlboro College and Columbia University. Until recently she taught in New York's Poets in Public Service program. She has received several fellowships and awards, including the John Masefield Award from the Poetry Society of America. Her first book of poems, tentatively entitled *The Misunderstanding of Nature*, is forthcoming from Graywolf Press.

Of "Interrogation," Black writes: "This poem was written almost ten years ago. It was one of the first times I consciously pushed myself right up to the Other and tried to explore that relationship. At the time I was reading Günter Grass, Milan Kundera, and Jean Follain. I was also involved in the drug culture in New York City, which was going through new agonies dealing with the terrifying disease called AIDS. We were in the thick of it, while at the same time I had begun my own spiritual struggle regarding commitment and addiction—a tangle I was trying to work through: how the Self becomes subsumed in order to honor, or be with, the Other."

STEPHANIE BROWN was born in Pasadena, California, in 1961, and grew up in Newport Beach. She has degrees from Boston University, the University of Iowa Writers' Workshop, and the University of California at Berkeley. "Chapter One" is from a manuscript entitled *[Italics Mine]*. She lives in the town of San Juan Capistrano, California, where she works as a public librarian. She is married and recently gave birth to a son.

Of "Chapter One," Brown writes: "When I wrote this poem I was ruminating a lot about the use of landscape and travel images in a narrative. Landscape can be a silent or not so silent character in a narrative. Such works as Ovid's *Metamorphoses*, the films of David Lean, the *fêtes gallantes* of eighteenth-century painting, and Henry James's novels use landscape as an unconscious reflection of a character's spiritual, ethical, political, or personal feelings. Travel narratives, such as the *Odyssey*, *Canterbury Tales*, *Gulliver's Travels*, or *On the Road*—or, for that matter, Michelin Guides—or, again, Henry James's works—reflect an era's Zeitgeist and the personalities that populate it. The characters in my poem bring their feminine experience, nationality, 'bookishness,' and so on, with them on their trip. They encounter a foreign landscape. They take a weekend jaunt rather than the long journey of another century. At the end of the poem the narrator asks herself a significant question akin to 'who am I?' I believe the asking of this question defines the contemporary personality. The asking of this question compels us to answer it, and, once we ask, we usually embark on an inward, perhaps spiritual journey to find the answer."

CHARLES BUKOWSKI was born in Andernach, Germany, in 1920. He was brought to the United States at the age of three, was raised in Los Angeles, and now lives in San Pedro, California. He has published forty-five books of poetry and prose. His latest book is *The Last Night of the Earth Poems* (Black Sparrow Press, 1992).

Bukowski writes: "The more said about a poem, the less it becomes."

HAYDEN CARRUTH was born in Waterbury, Connecticut, in 1921. He attended the University of North Carolina and the University of Chicago. He has been the editor of *Poetry*, poetry editor of *Harper's*, and an advisory editor of *The Hudson Review*, a position he still holds. He retired from teaching in the graduate creative writing program at Syracuse University in 1991. He has published twenty-eight books, primarily poetry, but also three books of criticism and two anthologies, including *The Voice That Is Great Within Us*. His most recent books are *Collected Shorter Poems 1946–1991* (Copper Canyon Press, 1992) and *Suicides and Jazzers* (University of Michigan Press); the former received the National Book Critics Circle award for poetry in 1993. Carruth's *Collected Longer Poems* is forthcoming from Copper Canyon Press.

Carruth writes: "Ben Webster was a musician whose work I enjoyed—and still do—as much as or more than any other. I've written about him a number of times in both poetry and prose. 'At His Last Gig' was written after I saw a documentary film about him produced by Danish television. Why did I choose to write it in such a difficult form, a sonnet using only one pair of rhymes in the first twelve lines? Well, there's no doubt I have a minor obsession with difficult forms and from time to time feel I must try my hand at them, but the main reason was my feeling that a fluid improvisation across the regularities of a strict form would make an appropriate homage to Webster. I tried to make the syntax varied and complex, as he did. And I like the simplicity of the final couplet after the formal intensity of the main development. Webster would have liked it, too. At least I hope so."

TOM CLARK was born in Chicago in 1941. Educated at the universities of Michigan and Cambridge, he currently teaches poetry and poetics at New College in California. He is the author of several biographies, most recently *Charles Olson: The Allegory of a Poet's Life* (Norton, 1991), and many volumes of poetry, such as *Easter Sunday* (Coffee House Press, 1987), *Fractured Karma* (Black Sparrow

Press, 1990) and *Sleepwalker's Fate* (Black Sparrow, 1992). *The Poetry Beat: Reviewing The Eighties*, his book of literary essays, appeared in the University of Michigan Press's Poets on Poetry Series. He is at work on a book of poems based on the life of John Keats. He lives in Berkeley, California.

Clark writes: "Not to presume to judge those who care to do so, I strongly feel it is not the poet's place to attempt to explain, augment, annotate, interpret or otherwise render 'user-friendly' his own poetry. To the contrary, I favor protecting whatever mystery poetry has left, and would also be so bold as to suggest that anyway the author is probably the one least qualified to speak on his own productions, given the unfortunate but inevitable effects of vanity, not to mention the equally inevitable shortfall between what one meant and what's actually happening in the work at hand."

KILLARNEY CLARY was born in Los Angeles in 1953. Her book *Who Whispered Near Me* was published by Farrar, Straus & Giroux in 1990. She recently received a Lannan Foundation fellowship. She lives in Los Angeles.

MARC COHEN was born in Brooklyn in 1951. Since 1986 he has been codirector of the Intuflo Reading Series, and is an editor of Intuflo Editions, a series of limited-edition poetry chapbooks. He is the author of *On Maplewood Time* (Groundwater Press, 1989). He lives in New York City.

Of "Sometimes in Winter," Cohen writes: "The poem was written on a Sunday morning in February upon my return from the barber. (Yes, Spike opens the Cooper Square shop on Sundays.) I began to piece together some stray lines I had written down regarding an unrequited love. Fauré's *Requiem* was playing in the background. For months it had been the first piece of music I listened to each Sunday morning. Perhaps the music helped transform the poem from a romance into an elegy."

BILLY COLLINS was born in New York City in 1941. He is the author of four books of poetry, the two most recent being *The Apple That Astonished* (University of Arkansas Press, 1988) and *Questions About Angels* (William Morrow, 1991), which Edward Hirsch selected for the National Poetry Series. Last year he was selected by the New York Public Library to serve as one of its "Literary Lions." Educated at Holy Cross College and the University of California at Riverside, he is a professor of English at Lehman College (CUNY). He lives with his wife in northern Westchester County.

Collins writes: " 'Tuesday, June 4th, 1991' started out as a kind of downhill, look-ma-no-subject-matter exhibition. Much of the poem was composed just as it occurred to me in 'real time,' to use a current irritant. I sat at the typewriter and began to describe the plain circumstances of this particular morning, and I soon found that the poem and the morning began to evolve in tandem. By the time I had shaped one notion into lines, then quatrains, some new sensation of minor occurrence would present itself for recording. This very chronicling of the uneventful—this scrivener's view of the world—quickly became the poem's ongoing, self-conscious interest. The poem's relaxed tone and its atmosphere of domestic ease may derive loosely from Coleridge's 'conversation' poems: a housebound speaker slips into a meditation that eventually leads him beyond the familiar surroundings of his room or garden. It was one of those lucky poems written without exertion, perhaps because I simply allowed into the poem whatever was going on around me, including young Felix, who entered it with his usual cool and now joins the company of Christopher Smart's Jeoffry and other distinguished literary cats."

PETER COOLEY was born in Detroit in 1940. He has published five books of poems, most recently *The Astonished Hours* (Carnegie Mellon, 1992). Since 1975 he has lived in New Orleans, where he is a professor of English at Tulane University.

Cooley writes: "Many of my poems choose me as their spokesman and arrive—after much waiting and labor—when they feel the moment is theirs. 'Macular Degeneration' came from my son's shouting 'not you' at me just as described. I had been wanting to write a poem about my mother's declining eyesight and the peculiar term for it which titles the poem. I see now that my son provided the epiphany and that the poem is about multiple vision, two sons', two mothers'. Incidentally, the coffee in the text is chicory, since we live in New Orleans where it's so readily available."

CAROLYN CREEDON was born in Newport News, Virginia, in 1969. She received the Paula Rankin Award for poetry from Christopher Newport University in both 1992 and 1993. She works as a waitress. "litany" is her first published poem. Her instructor, the poet Jay Paul, submitted the poem to *American Poetry Review* without her knowing it.

Of "litany," Creedon writes: "I am basically a waitress who goes to school. I had never written a poem before I took a poetry class two years ago. My teacher showed me how to gobble up details; that's why I like to cram as much as possible into every line. I knew I liked words: at least as much for their rich gushes and droughts, their sounds, as for their meaning. Jay Paul, who is my favorite poet, sent out my first poems to *APR*, and we were both a little stunned when one was picked. He's always right. About poetry, that is.

" 'litany' is a summary poem for me. It came in a singular rush about a week after my first lover had left me, finally. The words all poured out on this really humid August day when there wasn't any air conditioning and I was all alone with my bandanna and bathing suit. I wanted a sweaty immediacy; at least I felt it in the birthing of the poem. I tried to put a climax in every stanza *except* the last.

"I guess I try to write poems the way I think, and I 'think' a poem in long lines connected by lots of *and*s and *if*s—I kind of believe women naturally think that way. Ends of sentences and other pauses only come when we run out of time or hope. My 'questions' focus more on a child's attitude, a child's rage. The poem describes a baby's need to be cherished. Kids know better than their elders what a tenuous hold we have on anything.

"I tried to give a nod to God, especially a kid's God. The idea of a god here is meant to be mercurial—a god that can leave you, disappear. I think while I was writing it that the source of the destructive rage of the speaker wasn't Tom's departure but that of the God you know when you are a child. A God who is present but is passive and invisible and scary—powerful but not as alive to a kid as, say, a tangerine or dirt. At the same time God is never more real than when you're little and He's there, watching you through the sun. In 'litany' He is the one who will disappear in the 'swingset' stanza."

BARBARA CULLY was born in 1955 in San Diego, California, a place she still calls home. She earned her M.F.A. in poetry at the University of Iowa Writers' Workshop in 1984. She has been teaching creative writing and composition at the University of Arizona in Tucson since 1986. Her work has appeared in magazines including *American Poetry Review*, *Antioch Review*, and *Ploughshares*. "Repressed Theme" is from her manuscript *The New Intimacy*.

Of "Repressed Theme," Cully writes: "This poem is a meditation. I wrote it on the island of Menorca, where I spent the summer of 1989, having come to Spain by way of Italy and France. The tombs and artifacts at Tarquinia had startled me with a silence I carried in my drives along the Côte d'Azur and the Costa Brava. I was reading Jung at the time. The title 'Repressed Theme' is a phrase from Jung indicating the sources of complexes residing in the body, like springs or reservoirs, a way of talking about self or loss."

CARL DENNIS was born in St. Louis in 1939. He now lives in Buffalo, New York, where he teaches in the English department of the State University of New York. A recipient of a Guggenheim Fellowship and a grant from the National Endowment for the Arts, he is the author of six books of poetry, most recently *Meetings with Time* (Viking Penguin, 1992).

Of "The Window in Spring," Dennis writes "*E pluribus unum* (from many, one) is one of the more mysterious of national mottos, and I wanted to explore it here by trying to do justice to a neighbor, though the venture led me to concentrate more on the *plures* than on the *unum*."

TIM DLUGOS (1950–1990) grew up in East Longmeadow, Massachusetts, and Arlington, Virginia, and attended LaSalle College in Philadelphia. He began publishing his poems in the early seventies while living in Washington, D.C. In 1976, Dlugos relocated to New York City, where he soon established himself as a prominent younger poet in the Downtown literary scene. His books include *Je Suis Ein Americano* (Little Caesar Press, 1979), *A Fast Life* (Sherwood Press, 1982), and *Entre Nous* (Little Caesar, 1982). Throughout the eighties, Dlugos published his poems in numerous magazines and anthologies, including *The Paris Review*, *BOMB*, *Washington Review*, *Son of a Male Muse* (The Crossing Press), and *Poets For Life: Seventy-Six Poets Respond to AIDS* (Crown). He was also a contributing editor of *Christopher Street* magazine. Tim Dlugos died of AIDS on December 3, 1990, at the age of forty. At that time, he was pursuing graduate studies at Yale Divinity School.

Prior to his death, Dlugos compiled two manuscripts of his poems, *Strong Place* and *Powerless*. *Strong Place*, in which "Healing the World from Battery Park" appears, was published by Amethyst Press in 1992. *Powerless*, a collection of Dlugos's last poems (including his highly acclaimed "G–9"), is currently seeking a publisher.

David Trinidad, Dlugos's friend and colleague, writes: "Tim wrote 'Healing the World from Battery Park' in mid-July, 1984, two months after he'd stopped drinking. In many ways, the poem reads like an oath to the alcohol-free life he'd committed himself to: on a 'honeymoon,' as they say in support groups, he is eager to make amends to his estranged 'love,' to align his perception with an open-ended notion of 'God,' to experience 'a sense of peace.' Intoxicated by each 'deep breath,' he relishes his newfound empathy, for it connects him with others—strangers, parents, outcasts—and enables him to begin to mend.

"Shortly before he wrote this poem, Tim called to read me Joan Larkin's 'How the Healing Takes Place.' Her poem, also about recovery, describes 'how the eyes surrender their fear' and 'how the breath brings healing / to all parts of the body.' Tim was inspired by Larkin's sober poems and quickly followed suit. When he called to read 'Healing the World from Battery Park'—'hot off the press'—I was struck by the excitement in his voice and by his pride—he'd broken through, proved to himself that poetry was not only possible, but *better* without his crutch.

"Over the next six years, Tim retained his enthusiasm. Even as he was dying of AIDS, his faith deepened and his poems—many of them written 'in hospital'—got better and better. Letting go of earlier tricks and devices, Tim's poems began to move, as Jim

Cory has written, 'with fluid grace from observation to anecdote to recollection to philosophic insight.' 'Healing the World from Battery Park' marks the start of Tim's final phase as a poet. From the tip of Manhattan, the island he loved, he christens the qualities with which he'll forge his religion: trust, forgiveness, tenderness, light."

David Trinidad's latest book is *Hand Over Heart: Poems 1981–1988* (Amethyst Press). He wrote the introduction to Tim Dlugos's *Strong Place*, also published by Amethyst.

STEPHEN DOBYNS was born in Orange, New Jersey, in 1941. He is the author of fifteen novels and seven books of poems. His most recent novels are *Saratoga Haunting* (Viking, 1993) and *The Wrestler's Cruel Study* (Norton, 1993). His most recent book of poems is *Body Traffic* (Viking, 1990). *Velocities: Poems 1966–1992* will be released by Viking in January 1994. He teaches at Syracuse University and in the M.F.A. program at Warren Wilson College.

Of "Favorite Iraqi Soldier," Dobyns writes: "Like many people, I was deeply offended by President Bush's war against Iraq, a country that we had carefully armed and encouraged. The war seemed to exist to bolster Mr. Bush's presidency and turned the deaths of thousands of Iraqis into a sporting event. The photograph described in the poem was a photograph that I saw at the time. I find political poems very difficult, to write and often to read, but I feel that poetry needs to bear witness to the world rather than to the complications or shortcomings of the author's life. The photograph enabled me to construct a poem that contained my feelings about the war and the eagerness for violence and depredation that is so close to the heart of the human animal.

"Formally, the poem centers upon encounters with the letter 'T' (with a nod to its pals 'K' and 'P') which attempt to echo a violence that is eventually replaced by the peacefulness of the long 'O' when my hero reaches the promised land."

DENISE DUHAMEL was born in Woonsocket, Rhode Island, in 1961. She currently lives in Lewisburg, Pennsylvania. In 1993 her first full-length book *Smile!* was published by Warm Spring Press (P.O. Box 5199, Harrisburg, PA 17110). She is also the author of three poetry chapbooks, most recently *It's My Body* (Egg in Hand Press,

1992), a sequence of poems based on the lives of Barbie dolls. The New York–based actress Becque Olson performs Duhamel's Barbie poems in the one-woman show *This is Nothing New*.

Duhamel writes: "I began writing 'Feminism' after skimming my niece's Girl Scout handbook. It occurred to me that the Girl Scouts offer a systematic way to combat a girl's fear and distrust of the world, which starts early. Girls walk in groups, form troops, get badges, and protect each other. The handbook also lists games played by girls around the world, which reminded me of the regular *Ms.* magazine column 'Sisterhood Is Global.' I had just judged a poetry contest for the Girls' Club of America, and as a gesture of appreciation the organization sent me a 'girls inc.' mug. That red-lettered mug was sitting on my desk as I worked on the poem."

STEPHEN DUNN was born in Forest Hills, New York, in 1939. He is Trustee Fellow in the Arts at Stockton State College in New Jersey, and has received fellowships from the Guggenheim Foundation and the National Endowment for the Arts. He has won *Poetry* magazine's Levinson Prize and Oscar Blumenthal Prize and *Poetry Northwest*'s Theodore Roethke Prize. The most recent of his eight collections of poetry is *Landscape at the End of the Century* (Norton, 1991). *Walking Light*, a book of essays and memoirs, was published by Norton in 1993.

Dunn writes: " 'The Vanishings' was written over a two month period. The only circumstance worth noting about it is that our seventeen-year-old cat was killed by a dog during that time. Thus the reflections about loss—written at first with a certain retrospective distance—were informed with a greater immediacy as the poem neared its conclusion."

ROGER FANNING was born in Millington, Tennessee, in 1962. His book *The Island Itself* (Viking Penguin, 1991) was chosen by Michael Ryan for the National Poetry Series. He lives with his wife in Oak Harbor, Washington.

Fanning writes: "I wrote 'Shoelace' after reading *Vampires, Burial, and Death: Folklore and Reality* by Paul Barber, a grisly and informative look at rituals practiced in the past by Slavic peasants to make their peace with the dead. In my poem, the widow's response to grief (frantically unknotting her husband's shoelace, then tying it neatly) is more involuntary than ritualistic, but her underlying need for comfort and order in this chaotic world is probably the same as the peasants felt."

ALICE B. FOGEL was born in upstate New York in 1954. She teaches writing at the University of New Hampshire and lives on a farm with her husband and children. She attended Antioch College (B.A.) and the University of New Hampshire (M.A.). Her book of poems, *Elemental*, was published by Zoland Books in 1993.

Of "The Necessity," Fogel writes: " 'The Necessity' took a few years to come together, sitting close to done, but not enough, until I understood what it was trying to tell me. It began one early spring (which is really more like winter here) when the lambs were born. I remember standing in the doorway of the barn, and thinking about how loud the lamb's cries were; we had heard them from our bed. Perhaps because I was pregnant myself, I had earlier been wondering about the silence in which lambs are born (I've only ever known one ewe to come close to bellowing while birthing, and she had reason to, since she was small, her lamb was enormous and more or less sideways, and her uterus prolapsed as we pulled the thing out of her). I thought it must be a natural way to avoid predators, but even if that were so, this lamb had another level of survival in mind. I envied its urgency and focus, and as I kept repeating to myself—or to the great biblical night sky—'It isn't true about the lambs; they aren't meek'—I began to learn again that lesson that I always have to relearn: that it is necessary to have a voice, to make oneself heard, to tell the truth, to keep trying—to speak up, as Bruno Bettelheim says, at the first glimmer of awareness, and not to wait, out of fear or politeness, denial or despair. For me, the lamb dispels not only the myth that humility is more admirable than honesty, but our other myth, both political and domestic, that to speak out, to ask for what we need, even simply to express ourselves, makes us unlovely and undeserving, worthy of disgust and dismissal. We must stay awake, crying, listening and talking, until every hunger is fed. The triplet lamb lived."

TESS GALLAGHER was born in Port Angeles, Washington, on the Olympic Peninsula. She is a writer of poems, short stories, essays, and film scripts, and lives in Port Angeles. She has been advising on a film by Robert Altman based on short stories by her late husband, Raymond Carver. Her most recent publications are *Moon Crossing Bridge* (Graywolf Press, 1992), *Portable Kisses* (Capra Press, 1992), and *The Lover of Horses* (Graywolf Press, 1992).

Of "One Kiss," Gallagher writes: "I suppose this poem could be taken as a kind of fable of self-humiliation through the futilities—and fertility—of the imagination. As we know, the imagination can be used to amplify or to frustrate one's sense of possibility. In this case, the body itself is seen as a commodity which is either well equipped or not. The sign of intimacy in the kiss is likewise liable to be 'used up.' I meant the poem to be humorous, of course, and perhaps I get that effect by distorting what is physically possible—arranging this competition between a man with one cock and one with two. Maybe it's just silly enough to dislocate some views about where sexual power really resides—not in performance, but in the clear imagination of the relationship between sex and loving. The progression of the poem becomes really a set of slipknots that pull the reader past normal reasoning processes into that giddiness of delight poems especially allow when they are deft and witty.

"Since I grew up in a working-class background, the format of the poem may have come from working-class jokes, which can be rather crude yet are sometimes refreshingly frank about matters of sex. I think I also wanted to challenge American poetry's mostly puritanical elisions of sexual topics. There is a kind of unspoken agreement, 'nice poets don't talk like that.' I've begun to feel the need to go beyond certain courteous and conventional ideas of 'niceness' in order to open up important areas of mirth and inquiry. Both sex and poetry seem to be suffering from a dire case of seriousness these days, so maybe this poem is a small antidote."

ALBERT GOLDBARTH was born in Chicago in 1948. He is currently Distinguished Professor of Humanities at Wichita State University in Wichita, Kansas. *Heaven and Earth* (University of Georgia Press, 1991) received the National Book Critics Circle Award in poetry, and has been followed by *The Gods* (Ohio State University Press,

1992) and *Across the Layers: poems old and new* (University of Georgia Press, 1993).

In an interview that appeared in *Another Chicago Magazine* in 1992, Albert Goldbarth made the following remarks: ". . as I've said in letters when we talked about this interview, on principle I'm reluctant to talk about those kinds of things—what 'really' happened in my life, and what seems to 'really' happen in a poem. I don't know that the poems ought to be any stronger for the revealing of autobiographical information. I don't care whether James Wright has 'really' been in prison or not, when he writes a poem with great empathy about that experience. Peter Wild once said, 'It's the beer we're interested in, not the can.' I like that. And it's amazing to see how the po-biz industry encourages can collecting.

"Things like question-and-answer sessions, interviews, often leave me feeling kind of dirty afterwards. As if I've done the self-sufficiency of the poems themselves a disservice. When I go to a poetry reading, I feel that if it's a truly good reading, operating at peak level for both poet and audience, what I want to do is walk out of the room with the last words of the last poem ringing in my ears. I want to go home and feel my life is somehow transformed because of those words. Instead, inevitably, there's a question-and-answer session that reminds me of 'The Oprah Winfrey Show' more than anything, and those are the confused, weak, uninteresting, ego-filled words that are ringing in my ears. I know those things can occur on a level better than what I've just described, but most often they don't; and most often I'm sorry that all of those other gratuitous modes of po-biz expression exist. I don't care to contribute to them.

"These poems of mine . . . I see them as the best of me, given freely: the rest is just—'Breadloafing,' I call it."

From *Another Chicago Magazine* #24. Copyright © 1992 Left Field Press. Used with permission.

JORIE GRAHAM was born in New York City in 1950. She grew up in Italy, studied in French schools, and attended the Sorbonne, New York University, Columbia University, and the University of Iowa. Her books of poetry include *Hybrids of Plants and of Ghosts* (1980) and *Erosion* (1983), from Princeton University Press, and

The End of Beauty (1987) and *Region of Unlikeness* (1991), from the Ecco Press. *Materialism*, her new collection, is due out from Ecco in 1993. A recipient of a MacArthur Foundation Fellowship, she lives in Iowa City and teaches at the Writers' Workshop. She was the guest editor of *The Best American Poetry 1990*.

ALLEN GROSSMAN was born in Minneapolis in 1932. He teaches at Johns Hopkins University, where he is the Andrew W. Mellon Professor in the Humanities. His most recent books are *The Ether Dome and Other Poems, New and Selected* (New Directions, 1991) and, with Mark Halliday, *The Sighted Singer: Two Works on Poetry for Readers and Writers* (Johns Hopkins University Press, 1991). He lives in Baltimore.

Of "The Great Work Farm Elegy," Grossman writes: "This poem honors my nephew, David Grossman, a man of noble character who died of AIDS. He is one of the dead children in blue—the one who questions the speaker.

"By the action of this poem, the speaker (having exhausted all other means of explanation) undertakes to add to the work of life *The Great Work* by which we contribute to life the significance of life, and speak of it. The poem begins with an account of the declension of the world and a knock on the door.

"Thereafter, the (pedantic) speaker is engaged to the end with a fundamental explanation which he addresses to the fundamental question of children ('What did you mean? What!'). Early life and the end of life meet in the meadows and hay fields of the *Great Work Farm*, where the work of early life is the building (under the tutelage of God and the farmer of earth) of the 'golden house' (on the model of Adam's House in Paradise) and the work of the end of life is the singing of 'The Song of the Constant Nymph' (which recalls the first hours of the world, before time became time).

"The poem of explanation is finally the poem of the myth of explanation—the blank page, the page made blank by rain which each person of whom an explanation is demanded (that is to say, *each person*) addresses, and on which he or she inscribes the long letter of mind which she does or does not send, but which is in any case received—in any case blank."

THOM GUNN was born in Gravesend, England, in 1929. He has lived in California since 1954. His latest book of poetry is *The Man with the Night Sweats* (Farrar, Straus & Giroux, 1992). Earlier books include *Selected Poems* (1979) and *The Passages of Joy* (1982), both from Farrar, Straus & Giroux. His *Collected Poems* will be published in Britain this year and in the United States next year. A prose book, *Shelf Life*, is also scheduled for 1993. He teaches at Berkeley.

Of "The Butcher's Son," Gunn writes: "It's just a memory of the hot summer of 1945, when I went to live with my two aunts in Snodland, Kent. They had a milk-round, and the anecdote is really based on something my Aunt Mary said on coming in one day. I showed my aunts this poem, and they told me how the son made up for his return to civilian life, a lot of boozing, and sleeping with every woman he could, which was a lot, since he was very attractive. They were surprised I could remember he had red hair, but I always remember redheads."

DONALD HALL was born in New Haven, Connecticut, in 1928. He lives with his wife, the poet Jane Kenyon, in New Hampshire, and makes his living as a free-lance writer. His book-length poem, *The One Day* (Ticknor & Fields, 1988), won the National Book Critics Circle Prize in poetry. In 1992 he brought out *Their Ancient Glittering Eyes* (Ticknor & Fields), which expanded and revised his *Remembering Poets* of 1978. In 1993 the same publisher issued his eleventh poetry collection, *The Museum of Clear Ideas*. He was the guest editor of *The Best American Poetry 1989*.

Hall writes: " 'Pluvia' started, maybe fifteen years ago, as a lyric for music (William Bolcom had recently set three of my poems) but it failed to thrive. Three years ago I found the old version in a drawer and tinkered with it for six to eight months. Maybe its provenance accounts for the obsession with a dipthong. It pleases me to have written something, making sense, that resists paraphrase by absence of content."

MARK HALLIDAY was born in Ann Arbor, Michigan, in 1949. He lives in Philadelphia. Denied tenure at the University of Pennsylvania in 1990, he teaches English at Wilmington Friends School in Delaware.

His poetry books are *Little Star*, which appeared in the National Poetry Series (William Morrow, 1987), and *Tasker Street*, which won the Juniper Prize (University of Massachusetts Press, 1992). He is also the author of *Stevens and the Interpersonal* (Princeton University Press, 1991). He loves Bob Dylan.

Of "Vegetable Wisdom," Halliday writes: "I think the purpose of 'Vegetable Wisdom' is to establish a protective barrier between myself and the frightening attitude expressed by the speaker. Also, to provoke the reader into renewed rejection of the speaker's attitude."

DANIEL HALPERN was born in Syracuse, New York, in 1945. He is the author of six collections of poetry, including *Tango, Seasonal Rights*, and *Life Among Others*, all published by Viking Penguin. He has edited *The American Poetry Anthology* (Avon, 1975), *The Art of the Tale: An International Anthology of Short Stories* (Viking Penguin, 1986), and *Writers on Artists* and *On Nature*, both from North Point Press. He is the coauthor of a cookbook, *The Good Food: Soups, Stews, and Pastas* (Viking Penguin, 1985), and recently published a travel book, *Halpern's Guide to the Essential Restaurants of Italy* (Addison-Wesley, 1990). His awards include a Guggenheim Fellowship and a grant from the National Endowment for the Arts. He teaches in the graduate writing program of Columbia University. He is the editor of *Antaeus* and the Ecco Press.

Of "Argument," Halpern writes: " 'Argument' is meant merely to address the idea of maintaining the illusion of status quo at the gate of middle age. A poem that says it might be better to avoid the argument—conceived here as the conflict of a life together, whatever the admixture adds up to. But ultimately, via the play of metaphor, the conflict that dogs us through this life, be it illness, loss, or the gradual collapse of the body biology. Or: 'Argument' is a statement that supports the mechanism of pragmatic denial, cheaper than current therapy, a stronger shield."

PAUL HOOVER was born in Harrisonburg, Virginia, in 1946. He currently lives in Chicago, where he teaches poetry at Columbia College and edits the literary magazine *New American Writing*. He is the author of five books of poetry, most recently the book-length poem *The Novel* (New Directions, 1990). He has also written a novel, *Saigon, Illinois* (Vintage, 1988). He is the editor of *Postmodern American Poetry: A Norton Anthology*, which Norton will publish in the fall of 1993.

Of "Theory," Hoover writes: "In my ninth grade general science class I was introduced to the concept of refraction, the optical illusion in which objects placed in water seem to bend and thicken. I had always been aware of the principle, but having a name for it made the phenomenon all the more interesting. Likewise I've always been intrigued by effects like that of 'parallax view' or like the 'Doppler effect' (the warping of sound when passed above a certain speed). Part of the charm of these scientific oddities is that they can be experienced on both the everyday and metaphysical levels. The character 'X' in the poem 'Theory' refracts his own figure by making fish faces in a store window. In effect he rewrites himself with each new perception. His self-portrait is made casually enough. But he also drowns in the possibility that he is neither the image he sees, the self that sees it, nor the language that depicts both subjects. Like many of my recent poems, therefore, 'Theory' is ultimately about the dubious but inevitable narcissism of authorship."

DAVID IGNATOW was born in Brooklyn, New York, in 1914. A senior lecturer in the writing program of the School of General Studies at Columbia University, he lives in East Hampton, New York. In 1994 he will celebrate his eightieth birthday with the publication of three books: *Six Decades: The Selected Poems of David Ignatow, 1934–1994* (Wesleyan University Press); *Selected Short Stories* (Mill Hunk Press, Pittsburgh, PA); and *Meaningful Differences: The Poetry and Prose of David Ignatow*, a collection of essays, articles, and reviews edited and with an introduction by Virginia Terris (University of Alabama Press).

Ignatow writes: "In hindsight, I wrote 'Absolutely' at my unease with the underlying pressure for revelation with which most of us live, if I may single out myself as representative. Revelation in the sense with which all of us approach the problem of death. The approach takes many different forms. The one I felt needed to be aired is our fixation on science as the ultimate tool to apply to our everyday life and its experiences. It constantly beckons us further into the mystery in which we live, revealing a bit here and there, but eventually it leaves us frustrated and still facing the approach of our demise, in a welter of information that we are supposed to gain faith from as we search for revelation concerning our cause for being, our need to die, our hope for immortality. This is an ancient theme, but that it struck me was evidence that nothing yet has changed for us, except for our mode of search, and science offers us the latest in high-tech promise.

"The mood of 'Absolutely' is a blend of gentle satire and authentic anxiety about ourselves. It approximates, I think, what is left us to confront after the proposed and hoped-for revelation merges finally with our hopes in dying. But above all, I wrote this prose poem as an entertainment for myself. If it pleases others, it was doubly worthwhile."

JOSEPHINE JACOBSEN was born in Coburg, Canada, of American parents in 1908. She has published eight collections of poetry, two volumes of criticism, and three collections of short stories. In recent years she has received an award in literature from the American Academy and Institute of Arts and Letters (1982), an honorary fellowship from the Academy of American Poets (1986), and the Lenore Marshall Award for her book *The Sisters* (1987). She has had six appearances in the *O. Henry Prize Stories* anthologies. She lives in Baltimore with her husband Eric Jacobsen.

Of "Hourglass," Jacobsen writes: "I am not fond of analyzing my own poetry, preferring to leave the poem to itself and to the reader. I can best and most simply say of 'Hourglass' that it melds spring and death, empowerment and loss, and the joy, or distress, of differing human beings faced with present spring and imminent winter."

MARK JARMAN was born in Mt. Sterling, Kentucky, in 1952. He is a professor of English at Vanderbilt University in Nashville, Tennessee. He has published five books of poetry, including *North Sea* (Cleveland State Poetry Center, 1978), *The Rote Walker* (Carnegie-Mellon University Press, 1981), *Far and Away* (Carnegie-Mellon, 1985), *The Black Riviera* (Wesleyan University Press, 1990), and *Iris*, a book-length poem (Story Line Press, 1992). *The Black Riviera* won the Poets' Prize for 1991.

Jarman writes: " 'Questions for Ecclesiastes' began because I was reading Ecclesiastes and came to the second verse of chapter seven:

> It is better to go to the house of mourning, than to go to the house of feasting: for that is the end of all men, and the living will lay it to his heart.

I was struck by Solomon's philosophical point of view and by an irritation with that point of view, along with a sharp memory of how my father, a clergyman, made visits often to both kinds of houses, of mourning and of feasting, of grief and of joy. When I was a teenager, he occasionally invited me to go with him on visits to people's homes or to hospitals or homes for the elderly. His preface to those invitations was usually, 'Come along and learn something.' I learned a little bit about how much human extremity he saw, most of it in ordinary suburban settings, in greater Los Angeles, in the beach towns where his parishioners lived. The passage from Ecclesiastes brought back his evening task of going out and visiting people, part of his pastoral duty. But one event, the one the poem describes, which had haunted me on and off for years, returned with great force to my memory. I began rereading Ecclesiastes and writing the poem as I did so. I tried to bring passages of its Jacobean English, full of advice about the inevitability of human suffering, into the narrative I was constructing. Though it will seem far-fetched and grandiose, I realized I was conversing with Solomon, in a way. At the same time, I was trying to imagine a world of experience I had glimpsed but that my father knew intimately. I felt a mixture of outrage and understanding as the poem went down on the page in its paragraphs, rather like the paragraphs of the King James Bible in which verse lines are run together. When I came to the end of Ecclesiastes, I had come, too, to the poem's end."

RODNEY JONES was born in Falkville, Alabama, in 1950. He grew up in the country outside Falkville and has made his life in small cities in the American South and Midwest. He is the author of four books: *The Story They Told Us of Light* (University of Alabama

Press, 1980), *The Unborn* (Atlantic Monthly Press, 1985), *Transparent Gestures* (Houghton Mifflin, 1989), and *The Wars of Fashion* (Houghton Mifflin, 1993). He has received fellowships from the Guggenheim Foundation and the National Endowment for the Arts. *Transparent Gestures* won the National Book Critics Circle Award for poetry in 1990. Currently Jones teaches in the creative writing program at Southern Illinois University at Carbondale.

Of "Grand Projection," Jones writes: "Due to my own need to save face, I abandoned my study of mathematics long ago, but before I did that, I seem to have gotten the notion somewhere, perhaps in Number Theory, that no two ones are alike. As a result, I have been skeptical of the power of numbers, especially as numbers dictate public policy and consequently serve to make that policy legitimate. At the same time, I have been astonished and impressed by our cultural obsession with enumeration, with censuses, with all techniques and religions of computing and accounting, with our need to know an exact number to apply to the time of day, and temperature, and the amount of time we devote to sleeping, eating, and waiting in traffic, and, also, that these numbers somehow satisfy and lull us into a kind of mystical complacency and moral insensitivity, for while it is easy to say that there are seven billion of us, it defies imagination to trouble that number with human faces.

"Having said that, I am at a loss to explain why I should have joined the accountants and entered into the territory of a poem like 'Grand Projection.' Perhaps, at the back of my head, there was the faint ghosting of Robinson Jeffers's 'The Purse Seine,' for it was Jeffers who most perfectly distrusted the fabric of that altruistic net that society is always casting. Certainly I had, fresh in my mind, the images of a visit to El Salvador, and also the recent collapse of the stock exchange, which had been precipitated, to the best of my understanding, by a software program, which inadvertently recorded a magical number that signaled a number of brokerages to sell, and thus yet another tower of Babel was obliterated. I trust that all future projections will make some account for the accounting, and so I would account for the poem, allowing nevertheless that some small wild thing may have escaped the net of my ever-faltering omniscience."

DONALD JUSTICE was born in Miami, Florida, in 1925. He recently moved from Florida to Iowa. For his poetry he has received the Pulitzer Prize and the Bollingen Prize. His most recent book is *A Donald Justice Reader* (1992), published by the University Press of New England.

Of "Invitation to a Ghost," Justice writes: "Henri Coulette was a very fine poet and a dear friend. His death was an occasion I could not in conscience refuse."

BRIGIT PEGEEN KELLY was born in Palo Alto, California, in 1951. She has received the *Nation*/Discovery Award, the Yale Younger Poets Prize, and a National Endowment for the Arts fellowship. *To the Place of Trumpets*, her first book, was published by Yale University Press in 1988. She teaches creative writing at the University of Illinois at Champaign–Urbana.

Of "The White Pilgrim: Old Christian Cemetery," Kelly writes: "In a number of poems I've been using multiple narrative lines, interweaving narratives separate in time and space but related in theme, incident, feeling, etc. I'm trying to suggest a world of circular time in which seemingly disparate events are seen as part of larger patterns within a constantly recurring whole."

ROBERT KELLY was born in New York City in 1935. He lives in upstate New York and teaches in the writing faculty at Bard College. His most recent books are *A Strange Market* (Black Sparrow Press, 1992) and a third collection of fiction, *Cat Scratch Fever* (McPherson and Co., 1991). In preparation are a *Selected Poems 1960–1990* and a fourth book of fiction, *Queen of Terrors*.

Of "Mapping," Robert Kelly writes: "I'd driven with Pat and Marla Smith over the Taghkanics and been frightened by the aftermath of village crime in Pine Plains; on the way back Marla was talking about the ratio of flesh to fat in singing birds, the weight of music. Days later I sat in Green & Bresler's with Nisse Hope and Roger Deutsch; Nisse was playing with the Minka fountain pen Fortune Ryan had left as a gift on my door one day; she doodled contour lines that brought maps to mind, specifically the intricate Hungarian valleys in an old German General Staff map Christina Coyle gave me, that turned into the poem 'Cartography' dedicated to this same Roger, who later married this same Nisse, and off to Budapest with them. And I thought about contour lines, contours of our lives, desires, trying to write ourselves into the lives of other people. Body writing. I thought of the burgundy fountain pen I'd given Charlotte before she left for Seattle, a pledge of color, a pledge of writing.

"And that is what writing is. It comes from people being with people. God doesn't read, and gods hear nothing except the vina of Saraswati endlessly playing, until the last untuning of that lute at the end of life. Writing is always from and for. Writing is never static, in itself. (I think it's wrong to think of Ezra Pound as a sculptor, when his work wanted the kinetic, always, and saw more virtue in Disney than in Matisse. Unless sculpture, too, can not only stand there but can move. The dance. As Orpheus our master taught rocks to roll.)

"A poem is always coming from. And brings me with it, to say (as it seems I must always be saying) how it is to be me in coming towards you. Speaking is me turning into myself. For you. Always an almost imposture, as it seems, to speak. And here the poem is marked *for Charlotte*, to say that it is, in some special sense, for her, the act of reading like the act of writing, a thing devoted, to someone. (How can we devote a private act of public language to one special person? Rilke said: this poem is part of the possessions of this woman to whom I here inscribe it. But we have come a long way since then, we have no more ownership in those facts the words, and only the tenuous copyright. What an archaic thing the law is—nostalgic, brittle, pretty, full of pain, suggestive of privileges as remote as feudal rights. A legal fiction if there ever was one. We own nothing of what is said; otherwise a map would own the earth. Not owning a text, I can give it to no one. All I can do with it is what it does with itself: inscribe it on the face of things, and let it pass.)

"So mapping, making a map, seems a metaphor for all of our attempts to cope with the contours of our intimate experience by describing. By language, which is always a public matter. I found my way there (says the mapmaker), now you can travel too, and you will see wonders there, birds I forgot to see and caverns I missed, full of our unborn children talking softly and smartly by the fire, passing crystals from hand to hand."

JANE KENYON was born in Ann Arbor, Michigan, in 1947. She has received fellowship grants from the National Endowment for the Arts and the Guggenheim Foundation. She lives in Wilmot, New Hampshire, with her husband, Donald Hall. Her books include *The Boat of Quiet Hours* (Graywolf Press, 1986), *Let Evening Come* (Graywolf, 1990), and *Constance* (Graywolf, 1993).

Of "Having It Out With Melancholy," Kenyon writes: "Artists in general and writers in particular are far more likely than 'civilians' to develop mood disorders. I have long suffered from manic-depression, which in my case manifests itself as an almost unipolar depression. We all know what it is to feel sad. What I speak of in this poem is disabling, soul-crushing depression, the kind that puts your face in the dust.

"I am no more responsible for my manic-depression than I am responsible for having brown eyes, and I no longer wish to conceal it. For all of us whose lives have been damaged by this disease I attempt, in the writing of this poem, to make the best of a bad, bad thing. We do have the solace of art."

PAMELA KIRCHER was born in Marion, Indiana, in 1956, and was raised in Columbus, Ohio. She studied writing at Ohio University and Warren Wilson College. She has received three Ohio Arts Council fellowships and a fellowship at the MacDowell Colony. She earns her living writing software requirements and managing projects for the world's largest bibliographic database.

Kircher writes: "I wrote 'Looking at the Sea' after seeing an exhibition of paintings at the Columbus Museum of Art. The show featured seascapes by Winslow Homer and artists who followed him to the same coast. Every picture of the sea was different, and yet, I thought, the sea was nowhere in that gallery. Every picture was a picture of the self. Humans see subjectively or not at all.

"I wanted to show the sea objectively. I concentrated on a formal tone and a slight reversal of syntax to restore to the sea some autonomy and sovereignty. The personal pronoun 'we,' both collective and faceless, occurs twice. Yet the introduction of the human, framing eye instigates a breakdown in the line length, leading to the insistent, abrupt final phase that permits no explication. After all, only an emotional response is possible.

"Although the exhibit was filled with passionate, moving pictures by Homer and others, I purposely avoided describing any of them. However, the drowned boy in the poem was suggested by the show. The epigraph from Marsden Hartley accompanied one of his paintings in the show. Hartley had a friend whose sons drowned in the sea. He wrote a poem in response and his words characterized the impulse to attribute, or to wish, some emotion to the sea."

KENNETH KOCH was born in Cincinnati, Ohio, in 1925. He lives in New York City and teaches at Columbia University. His recent books include *One Thousand Avant-Garde Plays* (Knopf, 1988), *Seasons on Earth* (Viking, 1987), *On the Edge* (Viking, 1986), and *Selected Poems* (Random House, 1985). A British (and larger) edition of his *Selected Poems* was published by Carcanet in 1991. An operatic version of his play "The Construction of Boston," with music by Scott Wheeler, was produced in Boston in 1989 and 1990. A new collection of stories, *Hotel Lambosa*, was published by Coffee House Press in 1993.

Of "Talking to Patrizia," Koch writes: "Originally my poem had as an epigraph four lines by Patrizia Cavalli:

> Ma d'amore
> non voglio parlare,
> l'amore lo voglio
> solamente fare
>
> [But of love
> I don't want to speak,
> Love I want
> Only to make]

But I decided I preferred having Patrizia say this to her having already written it. Another epigraph I considered was a maxim of La Rochefoucauld:

Le pouvoir que les personnes que nous aimons ont sur nous
est presque toujours plus grand que celui que nous y avons
nous même.

[The power people we love have over us is almost always
greater than that we have over ourselves.]

PHYLLIS KOESTENBAUM was born in Brooklyn, New York, in 1930.
She has lived in California for almost forty years. She teaches cre-
ative writing at West Valley Community College in Saratoga and
is an affiliated scholar at the Institute for Research on Women and
Gender at Stanford University. Among her five published books
and chapbooks are *oh I can't she says* (Christopher's Books, 1980)
and *14 Criminal Sonnets* (Jungle Garden Press, 1984).

Of "Harriet Feigenbaum is a Sculptor," Koestenbaum says: "I
wrote the poem the morning after a night's sleep of only a few
hours. In the first draft, I used the details of terrible dreams I'd had;
in the second, I dropped them. Except for some tidying, I didn't
revise further, which is unusual for me, accepting that the paragraph
came together as it needed to. I am pleased that I kept everything
in the poem that was there in the first writing, except for the dream
details, and added nothing, because these people and events, only
they, belong together. One slightly wry fact: the Harriet Feigen-
baum of the title is a real sculptor, whom I'd read about—and the
name of one of my real teachers in high school, whose wife was
hospitalized, was Feigenbaum."

STANLEY KUNITZ was born in Worcester, Massachusetts, in 1905,
and was educated at Harvard. He has taught at Columbia, edited
the Yale Series of Younger Poets from 1969 to 1977, and served as
consultant in poetry to the Library of Congress for two years start-
ing in 1974. He was awarded the Pulitzer Prize in 1959 and the
Bollingen Prize in 1987. Collections of his poems include *The Poems
of Stanley Kunitz 1928–1978* (Little, Brown, 1979), *The Wellfleet
Whale and Companion Poems* (Sheep Meadow Press, 1983), and *Next-
to-Last Things* (Atlantic, 1985). Other publications include *Poems of
Akhmatova* (Little, Brown, 1973), *A Kind of Order, A Kind of Folly:
Essays and Conversations* (Atlantic, 1973) and *The Essential Blake*

(Ecco, 1987). In 1993 Sheep Meadow Press published *Conversations and Encounters with Stanley Kunitz*. A new collection of poems is scheduled for 1994.

Kunitz writes: " 'Chariot' was written for the occasion of a retrospective exhibition of the work of Varujan Boghosian at the Hood Museum of Art, Dartmouth College. The title is taken from one of Boghosian's constructions in which a bronze head (Orpheus) is mounted on an old wooden cartwheel. Boghosian's spacious studio in Hanover, New Hampshire, as described in the poem, is cluttered with a fantastic array of relics, souvenirs, cutouts, and artifacts that constitute the basic ingredients of his art of transformations."

DENISE LEVERTOV was born in Ilford, Essex, England, in 1923. She served as a nurse in World War II. She came to the United States in 1948 and became a citizen in 1955. Since 1981 she has been a professor at Stanford University. *A Door in the Hive* (New Directions, 1989) is her latest book of poetry. Other books include *Collected Earlier Poems, 1940–1960* (1979), *Poems 1960–1967* (1983), *Poems 1968–1972* (1987) and *Breathing the Water* (1987), all from New Directions. She lives in Seattle, Washington.

Of "In California During the Gulf War," Levertov writes: "For over a decade I have spent the winter quarter—January through March—at Stanford University. So I was in California for the beginning and supposed end of the Gulf War. The poem was written at home in Seattle during the summer, in the consciousness of so much continued suffering, especially among Iraqi civilians, and particularly children, as bombing damage and injuries were compounded by economic sanctions that deprived them of food and medical supplies. The war was indeed not 'over.' "

LISA LEWIS was born in Roanoke, Virginia, in 1956. She lives in Houston, Texas, and teaches English at Houston Community College. She has an M.F.A. from the University of Iowa and is completing a Ph.D. in English and creative writing at the University of Houston. She was a 1992 winner of the Poets and Writers, Inc. Writers Exchange and has also received awards from PEN/Southwest and the Academy of American Poets. She has completed the manuscript of her first book, *The Heart and the Symbol*.

Of "The Urinating Man," Lewis writes: "I had been reading about the work of the psychotherapist and hypnotist Milton Erickson, and I was interested in the way he treated patients by assigning them some activity, usually symbolic, or by supplying metaphors for their previous experience; he had little sympathy for the method of treatment in which the therapist helps the patient to understand his or her motivations. I had the idea that a poem about Erickson's work, as dramatic and metaphorical as it is, might free the poem to do what therapists are typically thought to do—to interpret the metaphor or the experience, to help the patient to understand. That's what I started with, an idea of the therapist as a kind of poet. But I doubt it's what a reader would notice about the poem."

THOMAS LUX was born in Massachusetts in 1946. He teaches at Sarah Lawrence College. He has received a Guggenheim Fellowship and has held National Endowment for the Arts fellowships three times. His most recent book is *The Drowned River* (Houghton Mifflin, 1990). A chapbook entitled *A Boat in the Forest* appeared in 1992 from Adastra Press.

ELIZABETH MACKLIN was born in Poughkeepsie, New York, in 1952. She works as a copy editor and proofreader in New York City. In 1990, she received an Ingram Merrill award. *A Woman Kneeling in the Big City*, her first book of poems, was published by Norton in 1992.

Of "The Nearsighted," Macklin writes: "Various pieces of the poem were written at different times—notes on the sights at the National Arboretum in April 1990; the hiatus incantation during some chaotic month in the early eighties—but the impulse to put them together, with that particular commentary, came just after the Senate Judiciary Committee hearings that famously involved Anita Hill's testimony against Clarence Thomas but also included Thomas's pretty wild display of fury at and contempt for the legislative branch. The poem, it turned out, had more to do with avoiding the subject.

"Later on, when I was making sure of my facts about the Corinthian columns, the Arboretum sent me an informational flyer, which began, 'In 1958 the east central portico of the United States

Capitol was carefully dismantled to make way for the marble clad addition. First proposed in 1864, the addition was considered necessary to correct the illusion that the cast-iron dome of the Capitol was inadequately supported.' I never did manage to work that in, unfortunately.

"What else? A certain kind of dittany (*Origanum dictamnus*) was once said to have the power to expel an arrow from a wound."

TOM MANDEL was born in Chicago in 1942, an American child of Austrian Jews fleeing Hitler. He was educated in Chicago's public schools, jazz and blues clubs, and at the University of Chicago. He has lived in New York, Paris, and San Francisco, and now resides in Washington, D.C., where he works as a consultant in computer networking technologies. His first book was *Ency* (Tuumba, 1978). Recent books include *Four Strange Books* (Gaz, 1990), *Realism* (Burning Deck Press, 1991), and *The Prospect of Release* (Chax Press, 1993). *Letters of the Law* is forthcoming from Sun & Moon Press.

Of "Open Rebuke (Concealed Love)," Mandel writes: "Sometimes a poet knows exactly what he means but not for long—for as long as it takes to write the poem but not much longer. My poem meditates on the fate of its protagonist and on a force that controls this fate. That force seems to be divine, and the protagonist appears to be engaged in the study of this enigmatic force—whose rebuke is open, whose love is concealed—and to be fascinated by it. Although this study may yield no understanding, yet the fascination itself is a kind of recompense for fate. In other words, my protagonist, however helpless, is not a stoic; he cannot be, for he is a Jew or stands for Jews. And this theology is clearly enough expounded in part two of the poem. In the narrative of part one, the brother and sister may echo the Song of Songs (they didn't in my mind as I was writing). In parts three and four, my protagonist, now a poet and willing to discuss himself and his fellows, seems to be enjoying the recompense of his isolation. He even takes pride in his difference. But in part five we see something else emerge, something unreconciled and abandoned but in contact with itself. The poem ends in a kind of fugue on the subjects of fragility and durability; its morphology shifts from a figure of Adam as Humpty Dumpty to an image of a jar, a container inevitably empty reminding us of what it once held. Did it ever contain more than the memory it holds here? The other day I happened upon Wallace Stevens's poem 'Anecdote of the Jar' where a randomly placed object works to transform an entire landscape. In my poem it seems the opposite: human beings do all they can, and it fits in a jar. The big inside the little—in Jewish theology that's divinity, the force I referred to above."

JAMES MCMICHAEL was born in Pasadena, California, in 1939. His books of poems are *Against the Falling Evil* (Swallow Press, 1971), *The Lover's Familiar* (Godine, 1978) and *Four Good Things* (Houghton Mifflin, 1980). His new book, *The Person She Is*, is forthcoming from the University of Chicago Press. He has also written two books of prose, *The Style of the Short Poem* (Wadsworth, 1967) and *"Ulysses" and Justice* (Princeton, 1991). He teaches at the University of California at Irvine.

McMichael writes: "The selection is from the early-middle of a book-length sequence. Written in the first person, these lines rehearse one segment of a twenty-year relationship between the writer and the woman he loves, a woman to whom he is not married."

SANDRA MCPHERSON was born in San Jose, California, in 1943. She teaches at the University of California at Davis, where she lives. *The God of Indeterminacy*, her sixth collection, was published by the University of Illinois Press in 1993. Previous books are *Streamers* (Ecco, 1988), *Patron Happiness* (Ecco, 1983), *The Year of Our Birth* (Ecco, 1978), *Radiation* (Ecco, 1973), and *Elegies for the Hot Season* (Indiana University Press, 1970).

McPherson writes: " 'Waiting for Lesser Duckweed: On a Proposal of Issa's' took five years to complete. It reflects my interest in botanical beings and also in trails, progresses, any point along which may be worthy of study and may illuminate. This poem began in Oaks Bottom preserve in southeast Portland (Oregon) and was enhanced by a visit to Hallam Lake, Aspen (Colorado). Lucien Stryk's translations of Issa's poems assisted the spirit and the eye of this poem."

W. S. MERWIN was born in New York City in 1927, and grew up in Union City, New Jersey, and in Scranton, Pennsylvania. From 1949 to 1951 he worked as a tutor in France, Portugal, and Majorca, and later earned his living by translating from the French, Spanish, Latin, and Portuguese. His books of poetry include *A Mask for Janus* (1952), *The Moving Target* (1963), *The Compass Flower* (1977), and *The Rain in the Trees* (Knopf, 1988). *The Carrier of Ladders* (1970) won the Pulitzer Prize. His latest collection, *Travels*, was published by Knopf in 1993. He has translated *The Poem of the Cid* and *The Song of Roland*, and his *Selected Translations 1948–1968* was awarded the P.E.N. Translation Prize for 1968. In 1987 he received the Governor's Award for Literature of the State of Hawaii. He lives in Maui.

Of "The Stranger," Merwin notes that he found a prose summary of the legend in question "and tried to tell it as the Guarani would tell it." The Guarani are rainforest Indians from the central section of South America, where Paraguay, Brazil, and Bolivia meet. "They are to South America what the Hopi are to the American Southwest: the museum, compendium, and storehouse for the spiritual life of that region."

SUSAN MITCHELL grew up in New York City. Educated at Wellesley College, Georgetown University, and Columbia University, she is currently the Mary Blossom Lee Professor in creative writing at Florida Atlantic University in Boca Raton, Florida, where she lives. *Rapture*, her latest book of poems (HarperCollins, 1992), was short-listed for the National Book Award. *The Water Inside the Water*, an earlier collection, was published by Wesleyan University Press in 1983. She received a Guggenheim Fellowship as well as a Lannan Fellowship in 1992, and is working on her third book of poems and on a collection of essays.

Mitchell writes: "Of all my poems, 'Rapture' is the most difficult for me to talk about. Writing it did not come easily, and eventually the difficulties of writing the poem became part of its subject. I really did feel as if I were translating from another language, a language that was purely physical, so that at times I seemed to be writing the poem with my body, imitating motions that were both inside and outside my mind. To write meant to match the motions of certain images. Or, as I say in the poem, 'an ocean of sound putting out stems / and branches of coral / which bend, break off, tempting / her body to match their motions.' I would drive along A1-A, the ocean road from Boca Raton to Palm Beach, and everything I thought was so architectural, so canyonlike—the limestone forms in my imagination were the only language I had, so it seemed hopeless that I would ever make the leap into the verbal. I was like the child in the poem, my nose and lips flattened against the glass of an aquarium, and inside the aquarium the poem was happening. All I could do was watch. Even my first move toward writing was physical. I began playing with blocks, two different desktop sets, a Roman and a postmodern. I was working something out spatially, the interpenetrations of structures that I imagined to be soft and living like corals. I think the interpenetration of forms eventually became the fluidity of pronouns in the poem, the way the 'he' becomes 'she' and the 'she' is transformed into the 'I' or narrator."

A. F. MORITZ was born in Niles, Ohio, in 1947. His books of poems include *The Tradition* (Princeton University Press, 1986), *Song of Fear* (Brick Books, 1992), and *The Ruined Cottage* (Toronto: Wolsak & Wynn, 1993). He has received an award in literature from the American Academy and Institute of Arts and Letters. His work was included in the 1991 edition of *The Best American Poetry*. He has lived in Toronto since 1974 and teaches English literature at the University of Toronto.

Of "April Fool's Day, Mount Pleasant Cemetery," Moritz writes: "Mount Pleasant Cemetery is a beautifully landscaped four-hundred-acre cemetery in the heart of Toronto, near the intersection of Yonge Street and St. Clair Avenue. For eleven years I lived in the area; Mount Pleasant was my park and its stones and monuments were part of my education in Toronto's past. Northrop Frye's house was close by and I'd sometimes see him in the neighboring streets carrying home a plastic bag full of milk and bread.

" 'April Fool's Day' belongs to my book about the city, *The Ruined Cottage*. Social engagement in poetry is often set against concentration upon the self; but the I is necessarily present as the means of engagement, and it seems to me that the poem must include both self and other plus the process and problems of their interrelation. 'April Fool's Day' is about something that happened and how I felt. It is about the irritated yet rebelliously self-assertive mode of self-awareness, the way it is compounded of love for and rejection of persons, nature, the city, and the way it is related to both the self-deluding and the reality-seeking aspects of our longing for the dead, the invisible, and the divine. This is a prime drama of all cities."

MARY OLIVER was born in Ohio in 1935. Her *New and Selected Poems* (Beacon Press) won the National Book Award for poetry in 1992. Among her earlier volumes are *House of Light, Dream Work*, and *American Primitive*, for which she received the Pulitzer Prize in 1984. She has lived for many years in Provincetown, Massachusetts, and continues to spend summers there; she now lives in Virginia and teaches at Sweet Briar College.

RON PADGETT was born in Tulsa, Oklahoma, in 1942. He is publications director of Teachers & Writers Collaborative in New York City. His recent books include *The Big Something* (The Figures), *Great Balls of Fire* (Coffee House Press), *Blood Work: Selected Prose* (Bamberger Books), and a translation of Blaise Cendrars's *Complete Poems* (University of California Press). He is the editor of *The Complete Poems of Edwin Denby* (Random House, 1986) and *The Teachers & Writers Handbook of Poetic Forms* (Teachers & Writers Collaborative, 1987).

MICHAEL PALMER was born in New York City in 1943 and has lived in San Francisco since 1969. He is the author of six collections of poetry, the two most recent being *First Figure* (1984) and *Sun* (1988), both from North Point Press. *Sun* received the P.E.N. West poetry award. A new collection, *At Passages*, will be published in 1993. His translation of Emmanuel Hocquard's *Theory of Tables* will appear soon from O-blēk Press, and the University of New Mexico Press will publish his *Selected Essays, Interviews and Talks* in 1994. He is currently involved in a dance collaboration with Margaret Jenkins, Rinde Eckert, and Paul Dresher, which will have its premiere in September 1993. He has received a Guggenheim Fellowship in poetry and a three-year writer's award from the Lila Wallace–Reader's Digest Fund.

Palmer writes: " 'Who Is To Say' is one of three poems ('Three Russian Songs') begun in a city on the verge of no longer being called Leningrad. A city suspended among its past and future fictions, fictions that seemed all too real, like the ghosts in every mirror. I was traveling with four other American and five Russian poets, and 'Who is to say' was one of the urgent questions we kept hearing. We were invited several times to the Writers' Union, then in the process of attempting to democratize itself. Its famous dining room, ornate and decaying, looked out over the Neva. The hallways were lined with framed photographs of Soviet writers, while in the basement loomed an enormous statue of Mayakovsky. The 'House of Tongues' in my poem is a composite of this and other interiors experienced on that trip."

LUCIA MARIA PERILLO was born in New York in 1958. She teaches at Southern Illinois University in Carbondale and spends part of the year in Washington state. *Dangerous Life* (Northeastern University Press, 1989), her first book, won the Poetry Society of America's Norma Farber Award.

Perillo writes: " 'Skin' was written sometime during the fracas over the display of Robert Mapplethorpe's photographs in (I think) Cincinnati. I had long been an admirer of his work, though it was a tangential admiration that originated in his being the portraitist of musician Patti Smith, a female icon of my high school days, which give the poem its backdrop. Though Smith isn't in the poem, I think she embodies the sort of abandon—and an ironic smirkiness at the degree to which society is still outraged by the body—that is supposed to be the spirit here.

"An ideal reader would understand the white lily that closes the poem as a reference to Mapplethorpe's signature image and not just some sort of romantic trope. But since Mapplethorpe isn't, technically, in the poem either, that lily will have to serve as his ghost."

WANG PING was born in Shanghai in 1957. She came to New York in 1985 and now lives in Brooklyn. Her poems have appeared in

Asylum, *The West Coast Line*, *New Poets* (Beijing), and several Chinese literary magazines. She has just completed a novel, *The Foreign Devil*, and is editing and translating an anthology of Chinese avant-garde poetry, 1982–1992. She is studying comparative literature at New York University.

Wang Ping writes: " 'Flesh and spirit' (the idiomatic phrase would be 'body and soul') is *ling yu rou* in Chinese ('spirit and flesh'). The reversed order of the two words reflects a fundamental difference between the Western and Chinese cultures. Until I came to New York City in 1985 at the age of twenty-eight, I had never owned a lipstick or a bottle of perfume, never heard of the words 'mascara' or 'clitoris.' It was only very recently that I began to understand my late grandma, a widow and a single parent for sixty years, and my mother, who gave up everything to follow my father to an island in the East China Sea, and who, in her disappointment and boredom, had an unsuccessful affair with a Navy officer. For too long, the pains and sufferings of the flesh have been taken for granted as a means of elevating the spirit. The repressed flesh of many generations screamed in my body and finally burst one day; I rushed to my computer and wrote this poem in twenty minutes.

"Things are quite different now in China. Everybody except a few stubborn poets is busy making money. People joke cynically: everything is for sale, even the Forbidden Palace and the Great Wall. One of my friends, who used to be an artist, advised me that I should become a businesswoman flying back and forth between China and America. If I lose this golden opportunity for material accumulation, he warned me, my children and grandchildren will curse me. I told him that I enjoy having money, but if it meant that I'd have to give up poetry to run after objects, I'd curse myself for the rest of my life."

LAWRENCE RAAB was born in Pittsfield, Massachusetts, in 1946. His most recent volume of poetry, *What We Don't Know About Each Other* (Penguin, 1993), was selected by Stephen Dunn for the National Poetry Series. Raab is the author of three other collections of poems: *Other Children* (Carnegie-Mellon, 1987), *The Collector of Cold Weather* (The Ecco Press, 1976), and *Mysteries of the Horizon* (Doubleday, 1972). He has received the Bess Hokin Prize from

Poetry magazine, a Junior Fellowship from the University of Michigan Society of Fellows, and grants from the Massachusetts Council on the Arts and the National Endowment for the Arts. He lives in Williamstown, Massachusetts, where he teaches writing and literature at Williams College.

Of "Magic Problems," Raab writes: "I had a friend who could do magic tricks—cards, coins, small disappearances. I was always taken in, and always asked how he'd done it. But he wouldn't say, insisting I really didn't want to know. The pleasure lay in being mystified. Once the illusion had been explained only skill remained. This provided the beginning of my poem, and led to other occasions in which explanations are desired, or invented. And then there are moments that seem to elude explanation, though we may take comfort in trusting that one exists. I wanted the poem to end with some such seemingly small occasion. The speaker hears a noise in the woods, and imagines a reasonable source—a rabbit, then the branch of a tree. Or perhaps, he thinks, something else—perhaps a man, trying to stand very quietly. This thought, of course, might lead in any number of quite ordinary—or quite ominous—directions. My pleasure was to let the poem end there, with those possibilities."

ADRIENNE RICH was born in Baltimore, Maryland, in 1929. Her first book appeared in the Yale Series of Younger Poets when she was twenty-one years old. *An Atlas of the Difficult World* (Norton, 1991), her most recent collection of poems, received the Lenore Marshall/ *Nation* Prize, the *Los Angeles Times* Book Award in poetry, and the Poets' Prize. Among her other collections are *Time's Power* (1989) and *Collected Early Poems, 1950–1970* (1993), both from Norton. *What Is Found There: Notebooks on Poetry and Politics* will appear in the fall of 1993. Since 1984 she has lived in California. She teaches English and feminist studies at Stanford University.

Of "Not Somewhere Else, But Here," Rich writes: "These poems were written very close in time, and share a foreboding about public events against flashes of something I'd call 'radical happiness'—that which reminds us of what is possible.

"A few glosses:

" 'What Kind of Times Are These': I was thinking of a place in northeastern Vermont where the Bayley Hazen Road, begun as a road to bring militia for the American Revolution up to Canada, breaks off to become a track through woods. Near it there's a meetinghouse of the Scottish Covenanters, a sect driven from Scotland by the Protestant church in the early nineteenth century, some of whom settled the area. The sect no longer exists but many traces remain in those parts.

"In the second stanza's second line I echo myself twice: from a poem called 'Blue Rock': 'No, this isn't Persian Poetry I'm quoting / All this is here in North America,' and from the title of another poem of mine, 'Not Somewhere Else, But Here.' The phrase, 'moving closer to its own truth and dread,' is adapted from a poem of Osip Mandelstam, as rendered by Clarence Brown and W. S. Merwin: #126: 'the earth's moving nearer to truth and to dread.'

"I didn't know till I was halfway through the last stanza that I was going to be paraphrasing Bertolt Brecht's 'To Those Who Come Later': 'What kind of times are these / When it's almost a crime / To talk about trees / Because it means keeping silent / About so many evil deeds?' Of course, the title followed.

" 'To the Days': The German/Jewish revolutionary, Rosa Luxemburg, wrote in a letter of 1916: 'Then see to it that you stay human . . . Being human means joyfully throwing your whole life 'on the scales of destiny' when need be, but all the while rejoicing in every sunny day and every beautiful cloud. Ach, I know of no formula to write you for being human . . .' "

LAURA RIDING (1901–1991) was born Laura Reichenthal and was educated at Girls' High School in Brooklyn and at Cornell University. She married Louis Gottschalk in 1920 and published poems under the name Laura Riding Gottschalk. At the end of 1925 she went to England, remaining abroad until 1939. In 1927 she legally adopted the surname Riding, Laura Riding being her authorial name until her marriage in 1941 to Schuyler B. Jackson, at which time she began writing as Laura Jackson and later as Laura (Riding) Jackson.

During her years abroad, spent mainly in England and Majorca, she wrote in collaboration with Robert Graves *A Survey of Modernist Poetry* (1927) and *A Pamphlet Against Anthologies* (1928) and with

Graves cofounded the Seizin Press. She also published some twenty books of poetry, criticism, and fiction, including her *Collected Poems* (1938), republished in an expanded edition as *The Poems of Laura Riding* (Persea Books, 1980). Robert Graves used Laura Riding's thought as source material for his book *The White Goddess*.

In conformity with the late author's wish, her Board of Literary Management asks us to record that, in 1941, Laura (Riding) Jackson renounced, on grounds of linguistic principle, the writing of poetry. She had come to hold that "poetry obstructs general attainment to something better in our linguistic way-of-life than we have." She regarded language itself as "the essential moral meeting-ground."

In 1979 a cache of more than two hundred early poems by Laura Riding—including "Makeshift"—was discovered. All had been written between 1920 and 1925 and only a few had ever appeared in print anywhere. In the months before her death the author prepared these poems for publication and entitled the volume *First Awakenings: The Early Poems of Laura Riding*. Edited by Elizabeth Friedmann, Alan J. Clark, and Robert Nye, the book was published by Persea Books in 1992. *Chelsea* magazine devoted a sizable portion of a recent issue to the newly discovered manuscripts.

In 1993 Persea Books published *The Word "Woman" and Other Related Writings* by Laura (Riding) Jackson and reissued the author's *Selected Poems: In Five Sets*, which had originally been published by Norton in 1973 and was long out of print.

Laura Riding was awarded the Bollingen Prize for poetry in January 1991. She died in September of that year. The Poetry Society of America presented a memorial tribute to Laura (Riding) Jackson in New York City in November 1992.

GJERTRUD SCHNACKENBERG was born in Tacoma, Washington, in 1953. She graduated from Mount Holyoke College in 1975. She is the author of *Portraits and Elegies* (1982), *The Lamplit Answer* (1985), and *A Gilded Lapse of Time* (Farrar, Straus & Giroux, 1992). She has received numerous awards, including the Rome Prize of the American Academy and Institute of Arts and Letters and fellowships from the National Endowment for the Arts and the Guggenheim Foundation.

Of "Angels Grieving Over the Dead Christ," Schnackenberg

has written: "The title is from a description of the Thessalonikan epitaphios in *Byzantium*, by Paul Hetherington and Werner Forman (London: Orbis, 1983). Hetherington proposes that the epitaphios, an orthodox liturgical length of cloth, was worn, perhaps, over the heads of priests as they approached the altar to celebrate the Eucharist. The epitaphios of Thessaloniki was discovered in 1900."

HUGH SEIDMAN was born in Brooklyn in 1940. *Collecting Evidence*, his first book of poems, won the Yale Younger Poets Prize (Yale University Press, 1970). His other books include *Blood Lord* (Doubleday, 1974), *Throne/Falcon/Eye* (Random House, 1982), and *People Live, They Have Lives* (Oxford, Ohio: Miami University Press, 1992). A three-time recipient of the National Endowment for the Arts fellowship in poetry, he has taught writing at the University of Wisconsin, Yale, Columbia, and Wilkes College. He teaches a poetry workshop at the New School for Social Research in New York City, where he lives.

Seidman writes: "As is perhaps obvious, 'Icon' was inspired by the unveiling of my uncle's footstone, which under Jewish law takes place within a year of burial. He had died a few months before my father, his brother.

"The first draft, though loose, had a seductive 'music,' which I was tempted to leave more or less intact. However, the initial energies lacked rigor, and a long series of drafts commenced, ending in the present case.

"The poem was, in fact, part of an ongoing push of poems on parents. A troubling push, insofar as it is necessary to move out from familiar emotional sources to new imaginative space. I suppose one can only hope that the language itself will rescue us from narcissistic immolation.

"This poem stands out for me, since I will always be a little sad that I had to let go of its first rhythms in favor of something tougher. But the solution to the problem of deformation of the medium is always an objective."

CHARLES SIMIC was born in Belgrade, Yugoslavia, in 1938, came to the United States at the age of sixteen, went to high school in Oak Park, Illinois, and attended New York University. His first volume of poetry was published in 1967 and fifteen others have since followed. He received the Pulitzer Prize in 1990 for *The World Doesn't End*. His most recent collections are *The Book of Gods and Devils* (1990) and *Hotel Insomnia* (1992), both from Harcourt Brace Jovanovich. In 1992 he published two books of translations—Novica Tadic's *Night Mail: Selected Poems* (Oberlin College Press) and *The Horse Has Six Legs: An Anthology of Serbian Poetry* (Graywolf)—and a book of musings on the art of Joseph Cornell, *Dime-Store Alchemy* (Ecco). He was guest editor of *The Best American Poetry 1992*. Awarded a MacArthur Fellowship in 1984, Simic teaches at the University of New Hampshire.

Of "This Morning," Simic writes: "I have to admit that I don't remember the circumstances or the writing of this poem at all. Ants visit us in the early spring. Long before the birds are heard in our woods, ants in my kitchen announce the coming of the new season. Otherwise, obviously, the speaker is lonesome and blue. 'Early in the morning, about the break of day,' says an old blues song. That's the spirit of the poem, too."

LOUIS SIMPSON was born in Jamaica in 1923. He is a Distinguished Professor at the State University of New York at Stony Brook, and lives with his wife Miriam in Setauket. He is the author of twelve books of verse, among them *At the End of the Open Road* (Wesleyan University Press, 1963), which was awarded the Pulitzer Prize, and *Collected Poems* (Paragon House, 1990). His works of prose include *Three on the Tower: The Lives and Works of Ezra Pound, T. S. Eliot and William Carlos Williams* (William Morrow, 1975) and *A Company of Poets*, a book of critical essays (University of Michigan Press, 1981).

Simpson writes: " 'Suddenly' is one in a sequence of more or less autobiographical poems in my new collection. The paragraphs about the export business and my being a copyboy on the *Herald Tribune* are taken from life, but Sylvia Cosulich and my conversation with her are purely imaginary. I think this is fairly typical of my poems: they are based in experience but then something happens that I haven't experienced. Unless this happens the writing doesn't interest me, and therefore won't interest a reader, and I jettison the sheet. Poetry as I see it consists of the life we perceive through our senses *and* a vision. If either element is missing it's just prose or mind-drift. I'm pleased with 'Suddenly' because it's a truthful account of what I was like as a young man and also shows how poetry comes into the mind, or seems to come . . . from beyond the self."

GARY SNYDER was born in San Francisco in 1930. In 1956 he traveled to Kyoto and took up residence in the Zen temple of Shokoku-ji. He returned from Japan in 1969. For the last two decades he has been living in the northern Sierra Nevada on the edge of the Tahoe National Forest, developing a mountain farmstead and working with the old and new settlers of the region. Since 1985 he has been a member of the English department faculty at the University of California at Davis. Snyder has published fifteen books of poetry and prose. *Turtle Island* won the Pulitzer Prize for poetry in 1975.

Of "Ripples on the Surface," Snyder writes: "I had been out on Sitka Sound learning how to read the water from Richard Nelson (and also, in Juneau, from Nora Marks Dauenhauer). The poem deals with the levels of play between 'nature' and 'culture' or, as the ancient Chinese Buddhists would say, 'host' and 'guest.' "

GERALD STERN was born in Pittsburgh in 1925. He is the author of eight books of poetry, including *Leaving Another Kingdom*, his selected poems (HarperCollins, 1990) and *Bread Without Sugar* (Norton, 1992). He lives in Iowa City, Iowa, in Easton, Pennsylvania, and in New York City, and he teaches at the Writers' Workshop at the University of Iowa.

Of "Coleman Valley Road," Stern writes: "This poem seems to imply a *second look* (and chance) at existence, and at human experience, which is the blessing we dream of and which may be at the heart of the artistic experience. The speaker—me, I guess—is a mile or so from the Pacific near Occidental, California, and stops his car near a high cliff where some sheep are grazing, slightly above the road that leads steeply down to the ocean. I had actually never been there before, but in the poem, I am recollecting sitting there among the sheep, rolling a cigarette in the wind and listening to the distant sound of the waves. In the third stanza I confuse the two existences because I am—then—sitting there in my car (truly my only visit) listening to the cello (waves) and observing the clouds and cliffs. In the fourth stanza I identify two distinct notes on the cello, one that of the Other (God, Fate, Time), one that of the Human ('like a voice,' the speaker, me). I think 'slight sagging' (God's pity; Time's exception) directs the poem, as do the last two words ('a shrieking'), and that the one relates to the other. I am just discovering all this. The poem was more or less a gift, that I wrote very quickly."

RUTH STONE was born in Roanoke, Virginia, in 1915. For the last three years she has taught creative writing at the State University of New York in Binghamton. She lives in Binghamton during the school year and spends summers in Vermont on the slope of Mt. Horrid. Her latest book, *Who Is the Widow's Muse*, illustrated by Phoebe Stone, was published in 1991 by Yellow Moon Press in Cambridge, Massachusetts. *Second Hand Coat*, published by David Godine in 1987, was reissued by Yellow Moon Press in 1991.

Of "That Winter," Stone writes: "Although I spent my early years in the south, I grew up in the midwest. I am still looking with an uneasy eye at my memories of those years. We were all exposed to the inhumanity and sadism of the Nazis (1933–1945). During the war I worked on *The Indianapolis Star* and was required several times to view confiscated Nazi films of the death camps. I became numb. Those years of fever and dread seemed to require more and more horror. 'That Winter' is a miniature, a reflection.

"Reading it over, I realize that I mention two novels, *Of Human Bondage* and *Crime and Punishment*. When you are writing, the maturation of your memory supplies images and symbols almost automatically."

MARK STRAND was born in Summerside, Prince Edward Island, Canada, in 1934. He is a professor of English at the University of Utah and has held a MacArthur Foundation Fellowship. He is the author of nine books of poetry, all of them either published or reissued by Knopf. His most recent books are *Dark Harbor* (1993) and *The Continuous Life* (1990). He was guest editor of *The Best American Poetry 1991*, which he worked on during his tenure as the nation's fourth poet laureate, in 1990–91. He received the Bollingen Prize in 1993. He lives with his wife and son in Salt Lake City, Utah.

Strand writes: "*Dark Harbor* is a long poem in forty-five sections. When I sent out the sections for magazine publication, I sent them out in groups of three, not believing at the time that the single sections could stand on their own. Sometimes they were titled, but most often they were called 'from *Dark Harbor*.' Though grouped together for the purpose of magazine publication, the sections are not necessarily together in the long poem, that is, they are taken from different parts of it. The principle by which I grouped them was simply whether or not they seemed right together."

JAMES TATE was born in Kansas City, Missouri, in 1943. He was awarded the Yale Younger Poets Prize in 1966 for *The Lost Pilot*. His *Selected Poems* (Wesleyan/University Press of New England, 1991) was awarded the Pulitzer Prize for poetry in 1992. Other recent books include *Constant Defender* (Ecco Press, 1983), *Reckoner* (Wesleyan University Press, 1986), and *Distance from Loved Ones* (Wesleyan/University Press of New England, 1990). He teaches at the University of Massachusetts and lives in Amherst.

Of "In My Own Backyard," Tate writes: "I hadn't been writing for a while and was looking around for a way into a poem. So I just told myself, 'Look around, old boy'; and the phrase 'in my own backyard' offered itself as a title and a way of taking inventory. For me the lesson learned, the discovery this poem makes, is the obvious one: Look around, open your eyes, wake up—the poem is right in front of your eyes."

JOHN UPDIKE was born in Shillington, Pennsylvania, in 1932. He attended Harvard College and, for a year, the Ruskin School of Drawing and Fine Art in Oxford, England. He worked for two years as a Talk of the Town reporter for *The New Yorker*, and since 1957 has lived in Massachusetts, as a free-lance writer. In addition to his short stories, collections of criticism, and fifteen novels, Updike has published five books of poetry. His *Collected Poems, 1953–1993* was published last spring.

Of "To a Former Mistress, Now Dead," Updike writes: "The poem is written in blank verse, and in stanzas of eleven lines. These shreds of metrical form, however loosely worn, help me feel suited up with sufficient ceremony to lay claim to the title of poet."

ELLEN BRYANT VOIGT was born in Danville, Virginia, in 1943. She teaches in the low-residency M.F.A. program at Warren Wilson College in Swannanoa, North Carolina, but makes her home in Cabot, Vermont. She is married and has two children. Her poetry collections are *Claiming Kin* (Wesleyan, 1976), *The Forces of Plenty* (Norton, 1983), *The Lotus Flowers* (Norton, 1987), and *Two Trees* (Norton, 1992). She has received grants from the Vermont Council on the Arts, the National Endowment for the Arts, and the Guggenheim Foundation, and she is a 1993 Lila Wallace Writing Fellow.

Voigt writes: " 'Song and Story' was one of the first poems written after I had completed a book (*The Lotus Flowers*) of largely narrative pieces. It began with the refrain lines and was, I suspect, a way of giving myself permission to return to the lyric, including lyric fragments and the musical 'variations' in *Two Trees*. The poem is also, to some extent, an argument with Allen Grossman's brilliant essay on Orpheus and Philomela."

SUSAN WHEELER was born in Pittsburgh in 1955. She has received the Grolier Prize and the Roberts Award, and her poems have appeared in *The Paris Review*, *O.blek*, *Sulfur*, *New American Writing*, *Talisman*, and the 1988 and 1991 editions of *The Best American Poetry*. A collection of her poems, *Bag 'o' Diamonds*, is scheduled for publication with the University of Georgia Press in 1993. She is the director of public affairs for Arts and Sciences at New York University.

Wheeler writes: " 'A Filial Republic' was written during my first visit to the Southwest. The disparate lives of Mexican Catholics (many of them Penitentes) and the white New Age spiritualists around Taos (and the significant economic gaps between the two), as well as an emphasis on isolation and 'the view,' challenged my ideas of personal responsibility and faith, and the poem resulted. It was cast as an echoing response to Alvin Feinman's poem 'November Sunday morning,' which in an early version ended, 'I sit / and smoke, and linger out desire.' (In the recent Princeton edition of his *Poems*, he adds a final stanza.) 'A Filial Republic' is dedicated to Alvin."

C. K. WILLIAMS was born in Newark, New Jersey, in 1936. He teaches at George Mason University one semester a year, and lives the rest of the time in Paris. His most recent books include *Flesh and Blood* (1987), *Poems 1963–1983* (1988), and *A Dream of Mind* (1992), all from Farrar, Straus & Giroux. *Flesh and Blood* won the National Book Critics Circle prize for 1987. In 1993, Williams received a Lila Wallace—Reader's Digest Writer's Award.

Williams writes: " 'The Gap' is from a sequence that is the title poem of my most recent book. The poems use the conceit of dream as a way of investigating various elements of consciousness, and of events and states of mind. 'The Gap' tries to deal in as unpreconceived a way as possible with the shifting cosmological emotions and needs of mind, with the generation of solutions to metaphysical questions, and with the process of the skepticism that negates these needs and creates new attitudes of thought."

DEAN YOUNG was born in Columbia, Pennsylvania, in 1955. He has been a fellow at the Fine Arts Work Center in Provincetown and a Stegner Fellow at Stanford University. His two books of poems, *Design with X* (1988) and *Beloved Infidel* (1992), were both published by Wesleyan University Press. He teaches at Loyola University of Chicago.

Of "The Business of Love is Cruelty" Young writes: "The title of this poem is pilfered from William Carlos Williams's 'The Ivy Crown.' It's one of those rare poems that came out practically finished in one draft, which always spooks and frustrates me a bit; usually I get a real sense of accomplishment messing endlessly with poems. . . . When I was a kid, I had this vast collection of monster models painted with sure elegance by my sisters, but when I finally got the Bride of Frankenstein, they had had enough and I was on my own. When I painted her hair, things got rather out of hand, which is usually what happens when I write. Even then, I felt the draw of an aesthetics of ruin, of loss of control."

MAGAZINES WHERE THE POEMS
WERE FIRST PUBLISHED

Agni Review, ed. Askold Melnyczuk. Creative Writing Program, Boston University, 236 Bay State Road, Boston, Mass. 02215.

American Poetry Review, eds. Stephen Berg, David Bonanno, and Arthur Vogelsang. 1721 Walnut Street, Philadelphia, Pa. 19103.

The Atlantic Monthly, poetry ed. Peter Davison. 745 Boylston Street, Boston, Mass. 02116.

Black Warrior Review, ed. James. H. N. Martin. P.O. Box 2936, Tuscaloosa, Ala. 35486-2936.

Boulevard, ed. Richard Burgin. P.O. Box 30386. Philadelphia, Pa. 19103.

Boston Review, poetry ed. Sean Broderick. 33 Harrison Avenue, Boston, Mass. 02111.

Chelsea, ed. Sonia Raiziss. Box 5880, Grand Central Station, New York, N.Y. 10163.

Colorado Review, poetry ed. Jorie Graham. 359 Eddy/Department of English, Colorado State University, Fort Collins, Co. 80523.

Epoch, ed. Michael Koch. Cornell University, 251 Goldwin Smith Hall, Ithaca, N.Y. 14853.

Field, eds. Stuart Friebert and David Young. Rice Hall, Oberlin College, Oberlin, Ohio 44074.

Fine Madness, eds. Sean Bentley, Louis Bergsagel, Christine Deavel, John Malek, and John Marshall. P.O. Box 31138, Seattle, Wash. 98103.

Free Lunch, ed. Ron Otten. P.O. Box 7647, Laguna Niguel, Calif. 92607 7647.

The Gettysburg Review, ed. Peter Stitt. Gettysburg College, Gettysburg, Pa. 17325-1491.

Grand Street, ed. Jean Stein. 135 Central Park West, New York, N.Y. 10023.

Hambone, ed. Nathaniel Mackey. 134 Hunolt Street, Santa Cruz, Calif. 95060.

Hanging Loose, eds. Robert Hershon, Dick Lourie, Mark Pawlak, Ron Schreiber. 231 Wyckoff Street, Brooklyn, N.Y. 11217.

The Hudson Review, eds. Paula Deitz and Frederick Morgan. 684 Park Avenue, New York, N.Y. 10021.

The Iowa Review, ed. David Hamilton. 308 EPB, University of Iowa, Iowa City, Iowa 52242.

The Kenyon Review, ed. Marilyn Hacker. Kenyon College, Gambier, Ohio 43022.

The Nation, poetry ed. Grace Schulman. 72 Fifth Avenue, New York, N.Y. 10011.

New England Review, ed. T. R. Hummer. Middlebury College, Middlebury, Vt. 05753.

The New Republic, poetry ed. Mary Jo Salter. 1220 19th Street, NW, Washington, D.C. 20036.

The New Yorker, poetry ed. Alice Quinn. 20 West 43rd Street, New York, N.Y. 10036.

No Roses Review, eds. San Juanita Garza, Natalie Kenvin, Carolyn Koo. P.O. Box 597781, Chicago, Ill. 60659.

The Ohio Review, ed. Wayne Dodd. Ohio University, 320 Ellis Hall, Athens, Ohio 45701-2979.

OnTheBus, ed. Jack Grapes. Bombshelter Press, 6421 ½ Orange Street, Los Angeles, Calif. 90048.

Ontario Review, ed. Raymond J. Smith. 9 Honey Brook Drive, Princeton, N.J. 08540.

The Paris Review, poetry ed. Richard Howard. 541 East 72nd Street, New York, N.Y. 10021.

Pequod, ed. Mark Rudman. Department of English, Room 200, New York University, 19 University Place, New York, N.Y. 10003.

Phoebe, ed. Jeffrey McDaniel. George Mason University, 4400 University Drive, Fairfax, Va. 22030.

Ploughshares, associate poetry ed. Joyce Peseroff; rotating guest editors (for Winter 1991–92, Carolyn Forché). Emerson College, 100 Beacon Street, Boston, Mass. 02116.

Poetry, ed. Joseph Parisi. 60 West Walton Street, Chicago, Ill. 60610.

Poetry East, ed. Richard Jones. Department of English, 802 West Belden Avenue, DePaul University, Chicago, Ill. 60614.

Poetry New York, eds. Cheryl Fish and Burt Kimmelman. P.O. Box 3184, Church Street Station, New York, N.Y. 10008.

Provincetown Arts, ed. Christopher Busa. P.O. Box 35, 650 Commercial Street, Provincetown, Mass. 02657.

Santa Monica Review, ed. Jim Krusoe. Santa Monica College, 1900 Pico Boulevard, Santa Monica, Calif. 90405.

Sewanee Theological Review, poetry ed. Wyatt Prunty. University of the South, Sewanee, Tenn. 37375.

Shenandoah, ed. Dabney Stuart. Washington and Lee University, Box 722, Lexington, Va. 24450.

The Spoon River Quarterly, ed. Lucia Cordell Getsi. English Department, Illinois State University, Normal, Ill. 61761.

Southwest Review, ed. Willard Spiegelman. Southern Methodist University, Dallas, Texas 75275.

The Threepenny Review, ed. Wendy Lesser. P.O. Box 9131, Berkeley, Calif. 94709.

TriQuarterly, ed. Reginald Gibbons. Guest editor for Winter 1991–92, Alan Shapiro. 2020 Ridge Avenue, Evanston, Ill. 60208.

Virginia Quarterly Review, poetry ed. Gregory Orr. One West Range, Charlottesville, Va. 22903.

Western Humanities Review, poetry ed. Richard Howard. 341 Orson Spenser Hall, University of Utah, Salt Lake City, Utah 84112.

The World, ed. Lewis Warsh. The Poetry Project, St. Mark's Church, 10th Street and Second Avenue, New York, N.Y. 10003.

The Yale Review, ed. J. D. McClatchy. P.O. Box 1902A, Yale Station, New Haven, Conn. 06520.

ACKNOWLEDGMENTS

The series editor wishes to express his heartfelt thanks to his assistant, Kate Fox Reynolds, as well as to Glen Hartley and Lynn Chu of Writers' Representatives, Inc., and to Erika Goldman, Sharon Dynak, and Charles Flowers of the Macmillan Publishing Company.

Grateful acknowledgment is made to the publications from which the poems in this volume were chosen. Unless specifically noted otherwise, copyright of the poems is held by the individual poets.

A. R. Ammons: "Garbage" appeared in *American Poetry Review*. Reprinted by permission of the poet.

John Ashbery: "Baked Alaska" from *Hotel Lautréamont* by John Ashbery (Knopf, 1992). Copyright © 1992 by John Ashbery. Reprinted by permission. The poem appeared in *The New Yorker*, June 29, 1992.

Michael Atkinson: "The Same Troubles with Beauty You've Always Had" appeared in *Ontario Review*. Reprinted by permission of the poet.

Stephen Berg: "Cold Cash" appeared in *The Kenyon Review*. Reprinted by permission of the poet.

Sophie Cabot Black: "Interrogation" appeared in the *Agni Review*. Reprinted by permission of the poet.

Stephanie Brown: "Chapter One" appeared in *American Poetry Review*. Reprinted by permission of the poet.

Charles Bukowski: "Three Oranges" appeared in *On TheBus*. Reprinted by permission of the poet.

Hayden Carruth: "At His Last Gig" appeared in *The Ohio Review*. Reprinted by permission of the poet.

Tom Clark: "Statue" appeared in *American Poetry Review*. Reprinted by permission of the poet.

Killarney Clary, "An Unlikely One Will Guide Me . . ." appeared in *Ploughshares*. Reprinted by permission of the poet.

Marc Cohen: "Sometimes in Winter" appeared in *Santa Monica Review*. Reprinted by permission of the poet.

Billy Collins: "Tuesday, June 4th, 1991" appeared in *Poetry* (July 1992). Reprinted by permission of the poet and the editor of *Poetry*.

Peter Cooley: "Macular Degeneration" appeared in *The Iowa Review*. Reprinted by permission.

Spoon River Quarterly and in *The Ruined Cottage* by A. F. Moritz (Toronto: Wolsak & Wynn Publishers, Ltd., 1993). Reprinted by permission of the poet.

Mary Oliver: "Poppies" from *New and Selected Poems* by Mary Oliver (Beacon Press, 1992). Copyright © 1992 by Mary Oliver. Reprinted by permission of Beacon Press.

Ron Padgett: "Advice to Young Writers" appeared in *The World*. Reprinted by permission of the poet.

Michael Palmer: "Who Is To Say" from *Epoch*. Reprinted by permission of the poet.

Lucia Maria Perillo: "Skin" appeared in *Ontario Review*. Reprinted by permission of the poet.

Wang Ping: "Of Flesh and Spirit" appeared in *The World*. Reprinted by permission of the poet.

Lawrence Raab: "Magic Problems" from *Shenandoah* and subsequently *What We Don't Know About Each Other* by Lawrence Raab (Penguin, 1993). Reprinted by permission of the poet.

Adrienne Rich: "Not Somewhere Else, But Here," comprising "What Kind of Times Are These," "Amends," "To the Days," and "Miracle Ice Cream," appeared in *Southwest Review*. Reprinted by permission of the poet.

Laura Riding: "Makeshift" by Laura (Riding) Jackson, from *First Awakenings: The Early Poems of Laura Riding*. Copyright © 1992 by The Board of Literary Management of the late Laura (Riding) Jackson. Reprinted by permission of Persea Books, Inc.

Gjertrud Schnackenberg: "Angels Grieving over the Dead Christ" and notes for the poem from *A Gilded Lapse of Time* by Gjertrud Schnackenberg (Farrar, Straus & Giroux, 1992). Copyright © 1992 by Gjertrud Schnackenberg. Reprinted by permission of Farrar, Straus & Giroux, Inc.

Hugh Seidman: "Icon" from *People Live, They Have Lives* by Hugh Seidman (Oxford, Ohio: Miami University Press, 1992). Reprinted by permission of the poet.

Charles Simic: "This Morning" from *The New Yorker*, August 10, 1992. Reprinted by permission; © 1992 by Charles Simic.

Louis Simpson: "Suddenly" was first published in *The Hudson Review*, Vol. XLV, No. 1 (Spring 1992). Reprinted by permission of the poet.

Gary Snyder:"Ripples on the Surface" from *Grand Street* and from *No Nature: Selected Poems* by Gary Snyder (Pantheon Books, 1992). Reprinted by permission of the poet.

Gerald Stern: "Coleman Valley Road" from *Bread Without Sugar* by Gerald Stern (W. W. Norton & Co., Inc., 1992). Copyright © 1992 by Gerald Stern. Reprinted by permission of the author and W. W. Norton & Co., Inc.

Ruth Stone: "That Winter" appeared in *American Poetry Review*. Reprinted by permission of the poet.

CUMULATIVE SERIES INDEX

The following are the annual listings in alphabetical order of poets and poems reprinted in the first five editions of *The Best American Poetry*.

1988
Edited and Introduced by John Ashbery

1989
Edited and Introduced by Donald Hall

1990
Edited and Introduced by Jorie Graham

1991
Edited and Introduced by Mark Strand

1992
Edited and Introduced by Charles Simic

Other books in this series are available at your local bookstore or by mail. To order directly, return the coupon below to Macmillan Publishing Company, Special Sales Department, 866 Third Avenue, New York, NY 10022.

Line Sequence	ISBN	Title	Price	Quantity
1	0-02-044182-7	THE BEST AMERICAN POETRY 1989 (paper) edited by Donald Hall	$9.95	
2	0-02-032785-4	THE BEST AMERICAN POETRY 1990 (paper) edited by Jorie Graham	$11.00	
3	0-684-19311-6	THE BEST AMERICAN POETRY 1991 (cloth) edited by Mark Strand	$27.95	
4	0-02-069844-5	THE BEST AMERICAN POETRY 1991 (paper) edited by Mark Strand	$12.95	
5	0-684-19501-1	THE BEST AMERICAN POETRY 1992 (cloth) edited by Charles Simic	$25.00	
6	0-02-069845-3	THE BEST AMERICAN POETRY 1992 (paper) edited by Charles Simic	$13.00	

Subtotal ____

Please add postage and handling costs—$1.50 for the first book and 50¢ for each additional book ____

Sales tax—if applicable ____

TOTAL ____

____ Enclosed is my check/money order payable to Macmillan Publishing Company.

Bill my ___ AMEX ___ MasterCard ___ Visa

Card # _____

Expiration date _____ Signature _____

Charge orders valid only with signature

Control No. [   ]

For charge orders only:

Bill to: _____

Ship to: _____

_____ Zip Code _____

Lines Units

Ord. Type [SPCA] [   ]

For information regarding bulk purchases, please write to Special Sales Director at the above address. Publisher's prices and availability are '

_____ Zip Code

PSL/PS'

to change without notice.